# OUT OF NOWHERE
# INTO NOTHING

# OUT OF NOWHERE INTO NOTHING

CARYL PAGEL

TUSCALOOSA

Book Design: Publications Unit, Department of English, Illinois State
    University; Director: Steve Halle, Production Assistant: Rebecca
    Meier
Cover image: Howardena Pindell (1943–), *Untitled #7G*, 2009, mixed
    media on paper collage, 9 3/4 x 8 inches; courtesy of the artist and
    Garth Greenan Gallery, New York
Cover Design: Lou Robinson
Typeface: Adobe Caslon Pro

This book is interested in memory, accumulating particulars, and retelling a good story. It is a work of nonfiction and fiction. Though it includes research and aims for veracity, the narratives ultimately rely on the author's version of events. The author has been, and could still be, mistaken.

Library of Congress Cataloging-in-Publication Data is available from
the Library of Congress.

ISBN: 978-1-57366-186-7

E-ISBN: 978-1-57366-888-0

For my mom, Margaret, queen of the unbelievable story

# Contents

*A woman must continually watch herself... Whilst she is walking across a room or whilst she is weeping at the death of her father, she can scarcely avoid envisaging herself walking or weeping.*

—John Berger, *Ways of Seeing*

*The point has never quite been entrusted to me.*

—Renata Adler, *Speedboat*

# OUT OF NOWHERE
# INTO NOTHING

# Lost in Thought

In the late hot autumn of 2012, I found myself living as a house guest on the thirty-fifth floor of a high-rise on the west side of Chicago in the weeks preceding a haphazardly planned road trip out east and a future I had yet to divine. It had been seven years since I last lived in the city, and I felt fully like the stranger that—according to the science of cell regeneration—I approximately was. In the mornings I would wake early and for several hours—sometimes unshowered and silent in the floating apartment, sometimes buried in the stacks at the Harold Washington Library, and sometimes perched in a Logan Square coffee shop—attempt to string together the curious twice-told narratives I had been collecting for months. From there, when stuck on some plot's logic or unable to liberate a sentence, I'd walk the city streets, pacing with the hope of recreating a clear mind. Mostly, though, my walking thoughts were less comprehensible than the best of those I could compose and instead I daydreamed strange associations, abstract anxieties, and bewildering, unintelligible images. My body in motion forced a certain mental distraction, allowing my mind to wobble between contemplating work, imagining travel, and watching workers cut city corners as they sped through frenzied breaks. Sometimes I would head east on Grand and cross the river toward State Street and mobs of downtown shoppers, the aroma of chocolate lacing the air. Others, I'd walk south and east toward Millennium Park or turn northwest from where I temporarily lived toward Humboldt Park. Back and forth I'd turn, zigzagging along new routes as though there were nothing so crucial to my survival as this continuous

movement. I discovered that Humboldt Park—known to locals for its massive summer festivals, Puerto Rican arts center, formal gardens, history of homicide, and "Little Cubs Field" (an exact miniature replica of Wrigley)—was named after the nineteenth-century Prussian naturalist, explorer, and geographer Alexander von Humboldt, a.k.a. "the second Columbus," famous for his extraordinarily detailed drawings of South American botanical specimens (predating the 1859 publication of *On the Origin of Species*), and author of the exhaustive five-volume treatise *Cosmos: A Sketch of the Physical Description of the World*, which upon further investigation contained such magnificent and comprehensive entries as "Starless Openings," "Magnetism," "Motion in Plants," and "Zodiacal Light." In von Humboldt's only trip to the United States, during which he stayed at the White House as a guest of Thomas Jefferson, he never once set foot in Chicago. Humboldt was a lovely and large park, fairly empty during the day save for dog walkers and joggers, and one could squander hours circling the tall grass and rambling pathways. Around and around the city I'd pace, each morning hoping to hone a certain train of thought by listlessly looping the Loop, walking Wacker, or maundering aimlessly up and down the Magnificent Mile. It was the end of summer and the start of fall and all around me were lumbering, driving bodies barreling toward work, this job or that—appointments, lunch meetings, meetups, conference calls, happy hours, cubicles, offices—good citizens, all of them, bearing their portion of the city's labor. Additionally, there were those souls with whom my own treading paralleled: the homeless, wanderers, mothers, drunk, ill, adrift, visiting, and unwillingly or unhappily unemployed. Only for so long, I was discovering, could one defend against the anxiety of time by senselessly orbiting. Virginia Woolf, who had clear rules about this sort of thing (one should always walk in the evening "between four and six," and in winter for the "champagne brightness of the air"), wrote that the "brain sleeps perhaps as it looks," in her description of the particular reverie or trancelike state street-haunting generates and it was during one of these walks that I recalled the work of Harry Callahan who, in 1950, had taken a series of mesmerizing black-and-white photographs of women's faces as he paced the streets of Chicago. The first time I encountered Callahan's work was during a visit to see my youngest brother, M., and his fiancée, L., in Washington, D.C. a few months after they had moved out east and before I planned to stay with them for a week in mid-autumn. This initial summer weekend was oddly haunted by the *as yet unexperienced* but looming future visit and what kinds of activities we would engage in when I returned that fall; while spending time together we found ourselves talking about what *spending time would be like* when, soon, we were finally (at long last!) existing in this (created, approaching) together-space, each conversation lingering over *what it would be like* when we were *in* the time we anticipated being in. One extremely hot day, in preparation, we walked toward Capitol Hill in search of a bus tour with which to see the city but were unable to find a line that wasn't overly occupied by other tourists and, dreading the sticky red seats and claustrophobia of the bottom deck, we helplessly, overheatedly wandered around the Mall, eventually ducking into the National Gallery of Art more for the benefit of air-conditioning than anything else. I drifted in marble darkness toward a basement exhibit—"I Spy: Photography and the Theater of the Street, 1938–2010"— knowing that it featured a few Walker Evans photos and discovered upon turning a corner two small walls punctuated with high-contrast inky portraits: excerpts from Callahan's "Women Lost in Thought" series. The first photograph to arrest my gaze in the dim haze portrayed a young woman's pale face stayed in three-quarter profile, her curly light blonde hair wild, pinned half back and illuminated by streaks of sun against a jacketed neck and shoulders; she inhabited a particularly remarkable heart-shaped face with swollen lips, carefully arched eyebrows, high cheekbones, and the start to a puffy cloud of exhaustion shadowing the underside of her eyes. The woman—caught close up, her head the foremost factor in the frame—had what can only be described as an absent expression, with perhaps a slight frown rumbling under the surface of her mouth and running parallel to a single bulky silver teardrop earring, her eyes indicating, in my mind, some sentiment sorrowful, vacant, and stricken. The shadows of Callahan's shots were darker than most, the effect, so I later read, of a decision to prefocus the camera (which would quickly sharpen the subject while risking a murky and imprecise background) and overdevelop the film for maximum density. The subjects in this series, all women, filled the frames completely, isolating them from the city and occasionally resulting in a cropped-off crown of the head or missing chin. The photos were candid, Callahan having taken spontaneously surreptitious snapshots as he roamed Chicago streets in search of

subjects without an identifiable expression. The women—because they had no inkling their picture was being taken; because their faces were vulnerable in the false privacy of a moving crowd; because their eyes had fallen flat, slack, and static; because their expressions were erased as the result of (what one gathers was) a concentrated mind; because their bodies were automatic, purposeful, and separate; because (for an instant, in passing) they inhabited not just the public theater of the street but also the nameless interior location in the brain where humans so often dwell; because they were uncomposed and decomposing, vacant, blank, and naked; because they were clueless and alien, apparitional, stolen—made compelling, unprotected subjects, uncannily physical while still void of the soulful spark one usually associates with portraits. Another photo in the series was of a middle-aged Black woman in a flat cap staring straight into the lens of the camera. Her expression was powerful and direct, steady and unswerving. One could not help but feel *looked at*, unconditionally present, as if suddenly—via this woman's point of view—the audience had become the object of attention or at least, I imagined, as if Callahan himself was worthy of consideration. However, one discovers by reading accounts of his process that any sign of recognition is a fiction; the photographs were taken with a long-range lens from a significant distance and all subjects remained oblivious to being witnessed or captured on film. As I waited for my brother and L. to find me in the museum, I examined another woman from the series, a woman who was grimacing—cocked chin, stretched mouth, profound frown lines scoring tiny tick marks on her forehead—in what would otherwise seem like a moment of pain or trauma, but (*by the eyes—one can always tell by the eyes*) was more likely an involuntary, un-self-aware spasm and I wondered, leaning closer, what my own face conveyed in repose (*while squinting at this photo?*), or what sort of tableau my body ordinarily performs when caught in thought in public. Although all of Callahan's portraits were black-and-white, the woman in this picture had what I assumed was chestnut-colored hair and her contorted, ugly mouth disguised the machinations of a reeling mind. There is no way of knowing, of course, simply by sight, what someone else is thinking. She may have been anxious or pleased, exhausted, or suffering some mood wholly incomprehensible to anyone. The truth is that unless captured on film there are few situations in which we see ourselves as we actually appear to others: unposed, unformed, unpurposeful and innocently twisted with monstrous tics or perplexing gestures. And yet, candidly rendered (as one might appear in a childhood photo or on others' social media), we make an uncanny shape, incompatible with the image of ourselves we bear in mind—an image created from years of staring into mirrors or glancing at our own unconsciously fashioned and placed mask in the reflection of shop windows. While looking at these women—trapped as they truly existed for an instant, unprepared and duped into a mood of public privacy—I considered how one cannot continuously manage their emotive surface and, mostly, that this lack of control is something to be grateful for. After all, humans are a vain and foolish species known for deluding themselves to the highest degree and imagining that, for example, they exert a vigilant rule over that billboard of the body—that one most essentially sensitive physical location—the *face*, which is the source of as much communicative potential as, say, language, and also the way in which we (superficially, perhaps, but importantly) involve the world. While inspecting Callahan's photos I grew curious as to how often we even notice the subtle transitions between our own public (composed, controlled, posted) face and our private (lax, lazy, hollow) looks. From that day forward this idea punctured my walking thoughts and I would sense myself revising an expression or stretching to grasp a quick glimpse of my liquid shape reflected in a passing pane or puddle for, like anyone, I was capable of extreme shallowness even in the midst of my most focused trance. One sticky September afternoon after I had returned from Washington, D.C.—while strolling west on Armitage in the direction of Kimball—this vanity (I had slowed for an instant to inspect the effect of my reflection rippling along a tinted taqueria's storefront) reminded me, *out of the blue*, as they say, of a horrifying incident in the fifth grade when my teacher, Mr. R., would delight in playing what I'm sure he thought of as an amusing joke in front of the class. Mr. R. would walk into the room or interrupt a lesson to exclaim: *Hey! Let's turn around and watch C. blush!*, at which point my face, despite any attempt to halt such utter humiliation, would ignite, causing crimson streaks to stain my cheeks from neck to eyelash. These days when the conversation turns—as it often does with my particular set of friends—to the topic of embarrassment or petty childhood cruelties, I am known to retell this anecdote, causing gasps of laughter and shock as listeners are rightfully appalled by a grown man poking fun at a little girl's—vulnerable, uncontrollable, mortified—face, and yet the (still irrationally wounding) tale almost always provokes similar stories from friends, a reminder that these maddening idiosyncrasies—such as, for me, my whole life the, I'll admit, not atrocious but nonetheless distressing *act of blushing*—which we find utterly reprehensible in ourselves can prove endearing and even occasionally captivating to others; love, after all, being the conscious decisions to dwell on a certain soul's particularities with care and intention. To love is to mesmerize and be mesmerized by—to pay attention—and requires maybe more than anything an enchanting narrative. One imagines bestowed upon each poor adoring psyche the ability to classify, like Humboldt's *Sketch of the Physical Description of the World*, their beloved's essential qualities in encyclopedic detail: "Variations of Laughter in Company," "Length of Frustrated Sighs," "Hunger Signs," "Party Jokes," "Sleep Heat," etc. A few weeks after I saw Callahan's "Women Lost in Thought" portraits I received a gift in the mail, a catalogue from the University of Arizona's Center for Creative Photography which showcased Callahan's work from 1943–45 (the years just prior to the series I was studying), including some of his earliest street photography. The friend who sent it had recently born patient witness to my fascination with the fact that the "Lost in Thought" portraits were all of women. I was convinced—or at least interested in making a case—that women have a considerably harder time exposing their "true" face in a public setting. My argument proposed that Callahan was attempting to engage the gendered implications of a woman's appearance while lost in thought; the break in her trained physical vacancy; the moment (so rare!) in which she *is not* or *does not feel* looked at. Although Callahan's photos were more than sixty years old, it seemed to me that I only occasionally ever saw a very particular type of *unmanaged* far-off gaze in the passing masks of those who identify as women. This blank expression is different from the slack, comfortable mugs of men or the obvious, signaling worry of a woman talking with a friend, hesitating at the door, or in some way reacting to the environment. One guesses how unusual it must

have been for Callahan to catch a purely contemplative state—
an undoing of the face or absolute relaxation of self-awareness,
a jarring *openness*—when so often a woman responds to the
sensation of (however subtle or projected) public appraisal, attention, or judgment. Many women learn to compose their
face from a young age, to create it, and to make it something
worth looking at (one can, for example, slacken the muscles,
paint new shapes, or arrange one's hair as a frame surrounding;
one can blink up brightly, sideways coyly, or demur and bat in
faux-worry) because to be stared at—to inhabit *a vision*—is
another version in this world of what love means. *And yet, and
yet, and yet* . . . how beautiful is the face when unproscribed!
How much one cherishes the undone, the damaged and gro-

tesque! Perhaps it was the lingering presence of these thoughts
that led me to wake one November morning after finally returning from my trip out east with a paralyzing fear of walking

outside or of being seen. Instead, I attempted to calm myself by monitoring the city from the thirty-fifth floor—a true bird's eye view—feeling the full privilege of that vantage, the extreme distance creating an apocalyptic sense that all of Chicago could disappear, literally, in the blink of an eye. In Callahan's photos I had observed what happens when a pedestrian forgets, when they break the plane of conveying. I had seen that a face, when deficient of sufficient communicative expression, leaves something terrifying in its place—a soul stepping into their ghost, *growing apparitional*—and abruptly found myself wondering why that other hero of Chicago street photography, Vivian Maier, had not—despite the brilliance of her work and recent popularity—been included in the list of men (Harry Callahan, Bruce Davidson, Philip-Lorca diCorcia, Walker Evans, Robert Frank, and Beat Streuli) featured in the "I Spy" exhibit at the National Gallery of Art. Of the abundant posts that pop up when one types Maier's name into a search engine it is upsetting to discover how many of them mythologize her life in such a way as to distract from the significance of her work. In the mid-1950s (shortly after Callahan had paced the very same city streets) Maier, then single and in her midtwenties, moved from New York to Chicago in order to nanny for a family of three young boys (and is thus described by some sources as a "Mary Poppins"-type figure as well as a "spinster" and "eccentric"), taking thousands of photographs over the following decades but showing them to no one. Her photos depict Chicago street life: a ticket taker veiled by the grill of the theater booth, the grim stare of a street guitarist, crowds lined up outside of a currency exchange, a man pretzeled in the sidewalk's crook, plastically manic children, gooey teenagers, a beautiful brunette bobbing through downtown traffic. Interestingly (or *dramatically*, so it is made to seem in much of the material I encountered), it was only shortly before her death that Maier's anonymous photos were discovered on the northwest side of the city (they had been retrieved from a storage unit she could no longer afford at the end of her life) by a young real-estate agent named John Maloof who—about two years later, after much detective work—was able to attribute them posthumously to their author. Since then over 100,000 negatives have been recovered from auctions and boxes although while exploring the various websites, photo blogs, and online archives now dedicated to Maier I will admit to dreading that her alleged *eccentricities*— her poverty, solitude, pronounced privacy, and lack of colleagues in the field—have distracted from the force of her work. Unlike Callahan, whose startling shots of strangers were exhibited widely in his lifetime, Maier never sought to publish and, for all we know, would have been revolted by the suggestion, perhaps even appalled by the attention her work currently receives. Further exploration indicates much speculation concerning her *sacrifices*: a decision to *give it all up* (and what is the meaning of *it* in this phrase?—a husband, publications, fame? a steady job? children?) for *the sake of her art* (as if life were a series of controlled preferences instead of, as we know, a distressing and desperate selection among available circumstances). As I read about Maier one morning from my temporary home my eyes loosened their grip on the laptop's text to fix instead upon the then-early winter mist which had begun to stick to the windows and hang in heavy drops, plumped by the field of fog approaching, calling to mind a vast and disastrous blizzard, a mask of ash and feathers. For those few months at the close of 2012 I felt like an actual material element of the weather: hypnotized by clouds for hours at a time, becoming rain formation. In retrospect I realize how frightened I was by my inability to focus on the present moment (or present sentence), a circumstance that walking helped facilitate. It's true that my attention has regularly resided in the far-off place where "lost" exists—a location in which pandemonium dictates and the linear progression of "real time" becomes just another layer in the brain's palimpsest of imagination and memory. That winter I would allow my mind to drift, to trace the slack ends of some abstract and ultimately irreconcilable detail and then to *drop*, or *turn*, or *fold* from the initial nothing, falling further and further into the chaotic quicksand of my consciousness until each day became a loosely translatable trance: association mixed with reading, fact, and conversation; repeated stories and half-invented discussions; ideas both entirely and practically hallucinatory; a lack of lucidity and logic; and an alarming infidelity to *sense*. Like an explorer negotiating new territory, my ideas were built slowly and mostly of wrong turns, sketchy records, and too-curious digressions. Moreover, I became interested in the idea that this perpetual interiority (*the location of "lost"? buried in thought?*) had always, since I was quite young, affected the veracity of my recall. For example, I am more likely to retain the wave-like music of the opening rhythms of *Their Eyes Were Watching God* ("Ships at a distance have every man's wish on board. For some they come in with the tide . . . ") than I am to recall a single conversation with my seventh-grade best friend, both experiences having "occurred" the same year in my life. Only as I've grown older has this condition seemed at all curious, primarily since the fragments of my so-called past are more often sourced from other artists' work, friends' anecdotes, scenes from old novels, or photos than they are from firsthand experience. It is rare that I reminisce about my own life without effort or assistance, and I have observed that when I write down the details or tell a story orally the instance survives longer, causing my lived experiences to gradually become versions of twice-told tales embellished with the structures of fiction. Later that month—briefly relieved of my paranoia—I once again braved city streets and discovered that the more I encountered great swaths of pedestrians (or, as Woolf would say, the "vast republican army of anonymous trampers") the more I felt an ecstatic distance from myself: a ghost in the company of ghosts, each dreaming of lives unlived. I wondered if Maier was motivated to take photos as a means of keeping certain facts "alive" forever, of stopping time or halting vast-but-hidden stretches of human expression. The loveliness of the possibility recalled me to the late 1860s phenomenon of spirit photos, particularly William Mumler's, which at one time had the effect of convincing a small portion of the population of the veracity of apparitions. My favorite of Mumler's images is his most famous: a portrait of Mary Todd Lincoln taken after both Abraham and her youngest son, Willie, had died. According to legend, Mary Todd attended Mumler's studio incognito, calling herself "Mrs. Lindall" and wearing a headscarf as disguise throughout most of the session. The exposed results present a firm, durable scowl marking Mary Todd's square face with a pretty, hovering "ghost Abe" standing behind her, pressing strong palms to her shoulders in reassurance. Lincoln historians speak to Mary Todd's interest in Spiritualism, describing how she hosted séances at the White House, visited Lily Dale (a popular Spiritualist retreat), and participated in events organized by her medium friend Mrs. Cranstoun Laurie. While this was unusual (some have used the word "crazy") activity for a first lady, I recollect from my own reading examples of psychics famous for accuracy and renowned for their apparently divine knowledge. During the decades following the Civil War there were countless clairvoyants engaged in the (then-lucrative) business of translating psychic messages from dead war soldiers to their still-living mourners. For these patrons every vaguely familiar fragment of language must have brought the deceased back to the present moment—briefly postposing their eternal grief—but like lightning striking the ocean at night, a swift blaze through the bleakness could only have further revealed the exact and baffling fathoms of unknown that existed beneath the surface. Moreover, the role of the medium was an opportunity for women to harness their perceptive intellectual authority in a somewhat public setting (séances, card or palm readings, magic, or fortune consultations) and also coincided with the then-evolving suffrage movement. Almost all of the successful psychics of the time were women and we can even see them now as having provided national grief counseling, social work for the masses following a tragic and terrifying war. These psychic testimonies and transcripts might serve as some of the first documents of the American public seeking women for skilled professional labor, acknowledging their reliable command over a specific thread of knowledge that wasn't homemaking or childbirth. I cannot help but wonder what sort of dissent these mediums might have disguised through the art of prediction or what a woman (educated, until then, in silence) would have understood of a stranger through modes of perception other than language. One need only look to Marina Abramović's now-famous performance piece *The Artist Is Present* to locate a contemporary example of purposeful physical presence as affecting experience, attention as transcendence. In the 2010 performance Abramović—perched on a rigid wooden chair and cast in "a square of light"—faced a series of anonymous strangers, one at a time, bearing the weight of their stare for as long as they chose to remain there. She didn't eat, drink, or move, sometimes for more than seven hours a day, seeing over 750,000 people over the course of the 736½ hour event (the longest solo piece Abramović has ever endured), allowing each participant to commune with her in front of a crowd of onlookers. The arrangement was fairly

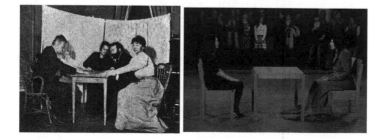

straightforward: an artist sitting across from her viewers; quiet, rapt. One morning, while studying a still photo of the piece online, I found myself wishing to consult the book on Abramović that a friend, A., had given me as a parting gift the summer before but remembered that it was regrettably buried in a far-away storage unit along with the rest of my library.

Instead, I watched how a time-lapse video of the event transformed Abramović into a mother, a lover, a nurse, and a maid; a starlet, a volcano, and a rebel. In interviews Abramović later revealed the immense physical and psychological energy the piece required to execute and it is not difficult to associate this role, both in setting and concept, with that of a medium: her stage the site of unclassifiable extrasensory contact and her presence requiring neither direct action nor speech to cause several sitters to claim profoundly religious and emotional experiences (resulting, in part, in a Tumblr site called "Marina Abramović Made Me Cry"). During the show Abramović donned, day after day, variations of the same stately gown in red, white, or navy with palm-length sleeves, a high neck, and what seemed to be a substantial wrap-around train, making even more dramatic her controlled and static expression, a clear contrast to the twitches, giggles, sobs, and fits inspired in her audience by evidence of an enduring calm. With a side braid and wan face frozen in an expression that was gracefully grave—as well as yards of weighty, eddying fabric—Abramović looked the image of a proper Victorian lady awaiting her suitor in the parlor, or perhaps Ophelia dragged out of the water. One would not have been surprised if, while dwelling in her own relentless concentration, Abramović experienced a feeling of levitation or hypnotism akin to magic. She described the feat as "a pared-down, long-durational piece that destroys the illusion of time," and it is simple to see how the room bore the weight of the weather that was Abramović's mood as she embodied an eternal circuit between artist, object, and audience. Some months later I discovered that a documentary about the performance had been made by HBO, but to be honest I haven't seen it and will admit that my favorite piece of Abramović's is still her 1978 film, "AAA-AAA," in which—for just under ten minutes, with a riotous face and vacant eyes—she screams the first letter of the alphabet at ever more alarming volumes into her lover's open mouth.

# Paul Revere's

I didn't watch the whole thing but I wanted to. It was over six hours long. When I walked into the room he was chest-deep in his prospective grave, digging diligently. In the video, to the side of the growing hole, sat a rectangular red plastic cooler like those a TV doctor might use to transport a heart or a liver. One assumed that his lunch was inside—a tuna sandwich? grapes?—packed by someone who worries. The digger, a man who looked about my age, was wearing a sky-blue T-shirt sans logo and yellow work gloves similar to those my father used to don before rotating dirt in the garden. On another wall of the gallery, in another room, hung a charcoal rubbing of the digger's future headstone. Once, in art school, my professor impressed upon the class Sir Thomas Browne's observation (appearing first in *Urn Burial* and later repeated by Sebald) that "a man may carry his own pyre." I can't recall the context. Too, a human body might hollow out their own grave, excavate a friend's skull, or pledge to someday appear beneath a reader's boot soles. Clouds blustered toward me from the distance in the image. I admired the colors, the concept, the plot. I touched my phone for any new texts.

•

The child might never have come out of the woods of his own accord. His family was attending an outdoor Boy Scout ceremony for his older brother and the little boy was playing sweetly with several children his own age in a clearing behind them. The boy followed another kid after a ball that was tossed to the edge of the field and when he arrived there, at the boundary of the forest, he stepped in. The mother and father, when they eventually noticed that their youngest son was missing, instigated a frantic search involving the entire troop of Scouts and the local police force. It took several hours to retrieve him. They combed the woods in organized clusters, calling his name at the top of their lungs, but the boy never thought—never even considered—that he was lost or in trouble. He had by then adjusted to the dim low glow of the forest, clawing shallow holes in the earth and chatting with fallen branches. He was, and still is, the kind of person instantly content being nowhere.

•

Steve McGuire thrashed through freezing river water—through floating chunks of detritus and muddy December ice, still wearing his bike helmet—until he reached the nearly submerged red Volkswagen Passat and with some difficulty dislodged a young woman trapped underwater in the driver's seat. He slowly swam her body back to shore. According to *Talk of Iowa*, when he revived a then-thirty-three-year-old Michelle Kehoe she shivered and sat up pleading: "My babies!?? Where are my babies?," as unknown to him there were two children left behind, buckled into the backseat. McGuire briefly wondered if his body, numb from the cold, was capable of diving in again when he turned around and saw—*only here, we later boasted, only in a small town*—that four other men had leapt into the frozen river and were saving Kehoe's young sons. On March 13, 1964, in Queens, New York, Kitty Genovese was stabbed to death with thirty-eight neighbors nearby, all supposedly in full knowledge of the crime as it occurred. Each of those thirty-eight witnesses remained unresponsive, not wanting, according to one onlooker, "to get involved." For years we retold the story of Steve McGuire as absolute proof of small-town kindness (until learning that Kehoe had been attempting suicide).

·

Directly before their first date (if you could call it that, which they did with starry eyes months later, although she hadn't imagined it that way at the time because *did he have a girl-friend?*—no one would tell) she fainted hard into the arms of a hospital nurse. It took several moments longer than it should have to revive her. She absented her body, and when she came to after a long and tangled while her mind was vacant: she couldn't recall her name, where she was, or anything that had occurred before that instant. She speculated that she had briefly died. In a cold sweat, clammy and confused, and having greatly alarmed the worried nurse, she stood up and walked out the door, then continued more than a mile in the blazing summer sun to meet him at a dive bar over on Market. The woman was polite and had thought it unseemly to cancel with such short notice.

•

We forget nothing. When one person does, we remind them. In this bar's booth, washed up from different cities, separate institutions, various affairs—here perhaps at first for school, then just sticking around or returned after some boring job or dirty split—our entire purpose, our total responsibility, it seems, is to remain in a constant state of telling—repeating this story or that; maintaining the notorious gory details; keeping histories alive, afloat, aloft, within so-called *earshot* (terrible gossip that it is); performing dramatic finales—with the hope that someday these stories might explain us.

•

It was Halloween night and D.'s girlfriend had thrown a party at the house she shared with two roommates on Church Street. They dressed as Stevie Nicks and Mick Fleetwood, posing in front of a printed-out replica of the *Rumors* cover. Someone had smashed a beer bottle in the bathroom, girls were getting groped in corners, and as D. and his girlfriend left around three in the morning they spotted a roommate gleefully tossing the splintered limbs of a dining room table into the flaming fireplace. When D. got out of the car at his apartment—a first-floor unit on the corner of Market and Governor—he halted on the path that led to his porch, glimpsing in the partial dark a curled-up shape—*a body?*—propped against his front door. He realized that the phantom was in fact a passed-out undergrad who had stumbled into the wrong place, presumably assuming in his wasted state (as students regularly did), that this was *his* home. D. shook the young man's shoulders and asked if he was alright; the girlfriend watched from a bottom step. The kid wore only a T-shirt and jeans even though at that late point, and in that season, it was extremely cold and close to freezing. He was conscious but staring at nothing, not responsive, not even, she noticed, wearing a costume. Regardless of what anyone said that night—D., the girlfriend, the police, the EMT—the young man just flashed a feral grin and refused to answer. Who knew, they said to each other, next semester he could be in one of their classes.

•

This morning in a high-rise building in Chicago I watched a man crawl down the ladder beneath a stopped elevator and into the mysterious underbelly of the interior to fetch the car keys of a woman who had dropped them in the slim one-inch crack between sliding door and tile floor. There are some things I am vigilant about: minding the gap, crossing the street, slowing down, holding on.

•

Her siblings had in common a sort of recognition problem. Whenever they were charged with the task of collecting someone at the airport, especially a close friend or loved one, each would panic, concurrently losing all understanding or memory of what that person looked like. In Washington, D.C. they attempted to pick up a small Mexican man whom they assumed was their mother. Another time, in Florida, they waved to every friendly gentleman with a sand-colored beard who might have been their brother. Individually it proved a problem, but together they were hopeless. A friend, the mom of a toddler, explained that she experienced a similar anxiety when leaving her son at daycare. She worried that when she returned at the end of the day she would have lost the ability to identify her child, that he would have transformed beyond recognition, or that all of the children would look the same. She learned, she said, to put some psychic distance between herself and her fear, to search for the tiny human that most resembled her husband.

.

A misogynist man employee, the woman coordinator said, was upset that she hadn't rehired him after years of offensive behavior. So was the other one. They both wrote threatening emails, one referring to the woman in a correspondence cc'd to her boss as "cold," "patronizing," and "bureaucratic." Abuses of this nature weren't new, not even terribly exciting, but in this case the office staff agreed that justice had been served: the man was an infamous bully whose bald head and shiny skin made him look like a penis. The other jerk looked like a thumb.

.

The magic of living in a small town is that people still, if reluctantly, converse with one another. At times this constant talk—manifesting as drone, whir, buzz, or hum—becomes claustrophobic: all that data, opinion, hearsay, history, gossip. Living in such a place can feel like being trapped in an elevator with a mob of toddlers. Like being one of a hundred peasants in a late Renaissance landscape. Tonight, we invent random rumors to test how swiftly they will ricochet: Carver Stadium was named after Raymond; Kurt Vonnegut once worked at Pagliai's; the tastiest pizza can be found at I.C. Ugly's. This town has a remarkable memory; stories congregate and compress—grow dense, tangential, complex—seeming to levitate above the crowd as an imposing mass, a *third thing* that one is required to contribute to, and—like twine for a nest or facts in a census—this data is meticulously gathered and archived. It's true, we know about your arrest record. We're familiar with your nasty divorce, and we're aware of the evening you shot down multiple streetlights with a BB gun. We know you made out with a psychopath. It's no secret you lied about rehab; some of us still recall the day you ate mushrooms and thought a vulture was descending to devour you. We know, perhaps better than you do, who you really love—your *one and only*—but are also conscious of your crush. We gave you tips on handling that rash. We supported you after the crash. We were there when your ex-boyfriend made you vomit up a pop-top because he feared it would cut up your stomach.

•

You get back to work. You make notes for a hypothetical essay: a study of Kurt Schwitters's *Merzbau* and other grottos, caves, hideouts, eccentric and protected made spaces. *Merzbau* and psychosis. *Merzbau* and childhood. *Merzbau* and the fort. Mostly: obsession. You will engineer your own replica of *Merzbau* (performance art and claustrophobic sculpture as research! no associates allowed in or out!). Instead of incorporating white plaster sections, bus tickets, old wire, doll heads, scraps of newsprint, and poems, you will decorate your space with pebbles from the cemetery, phone chargers, a skull-and-crossbones hand towel, kalimotxo, triangles, and a pile of miniature speedboats. You will build a moat. You will continue in a self-made facsimile *Merzbau* until death, bombing, or memo. The bibliography will include strident memorized screaming recitals of songs by the Baroness Elsa von Freytag-Loringhoven, Nina Simone, and coyote howl accompanied by the percussion of fork tines beat against a clean tin bean can.

•

"I'm trying . . ." the ex would purr prettily, believing himself at three or four in the morning, drunk, high, blacked-out, as they leaned against each other in front of Mercy making jokes about the sign that said EMERGENCY. "What *more* can I do?" Well, she'd think, holding the torn corner of his ratty leather jacket, not wanting to know, but knowing—(of course knowing!)—that the answer was *a lot*.

•

M. leans in conspiratorially; she manages the only great restaurant in town, the one on Linn Street across from the paper, the one with the gorgeous waitstaff. We go to their theme parties, leave big tips, and try foolishly to seduce them. Unlike writers, you see, they have jobs. "My *mother*," M. confesses, after telling a funny story involving a miscommunication at the train station, "won't stop eating gummy bears. They're making her *sick*. She's posted signs all around the house, on the mirrors, the furniture, the doors, instructing: NO MORE GUMMIES!" I laugh out loud. The buildings in this town used to be other things. Mostly hospitals.

•

Everyone shares a therapist. This means that we are obligated to manipulate stories when discussing one or another of the people the therapist also sees, most of whom happen to be the very people we wish to speak about, the very people who are making us ill. Pills lace the water. Tableaus of mental illness appear everywhere. On our couches, in the booth, walking slowly, glancing down, we are swallowing Klonopin, Xanax, Zoloft, Paxil, Nardil, Adderall, Ativan, Dexedrine, Abilify, lithium, and Zyprexa. The songs we hum are sad songs. For a year now there has been a pronounced gas leak in the apartment where we congregate for late-night dance parties. Someone passes out on the lawn. Occasionally the medicine helps, but mostly it is the process that confuses things: we are continually finding doctors, leaving messages, calling back, driving to the pharmacy, feeling better, slowly plateauing, definitely drowning, looking like shit, mixing medications, drinking too much, developing addictions, sharing prescriptions, stealing drugs, lying to loved ones, and in search of better insurance. We are barely ever "ourselves," and our personalities are verbal in the worst ways. We are suffering from predictable side effects. Once, many years ago—before her first book, her teaching job, and the birth of her now-young son—L. discovered and promptly popped a random pill she found on the fuzzy floor of Paul Revere's women's bathroom. It was a pizza shop. She returned to the table and we all stared at her beautiful face, waiting patiently for something to happen.

.

Someone calls me a bitch. It's "a joke." At the front table, by the window, flush in neon, the lot of us are some mix of bored, depressed, drunk, hungry, and pregnant. I walk outside through the back door and cry for a while against a thick brick wall with the phrase "WHITE DEVIL" spray-painted in scrubbed black letters as tall as I am. After a bit I go back inside. I find my chair, sip a drink, and reenter the conversation. Everything is exactly as I'd left it.

.

Three days before she returned to town—invited by her boyfriend to live with him and be his love in a four-bedroom house on her then-favorite street in the world (Ronalds) with a carpeted attic, fifties style breakfast nook, soft morning light, and lemon walls—he overdosed on opiates and nearly died. He stole some of her money; they broke the lease. But still, hadn't he taught her to two-step? She chose to continue existing anyway. Some questions lingered. When should she have taken him to the hospital? When should she have called the police?

•

In this episode of *The Real Housewives of New Jersey* the cast has gone to a castle to sort things out. The characters keep mentioning trust falls. Even though she was invited, Jacqueline has decided not to join because (so she says straight into the camera) she's "so over it." The group counselor looks upset. The entire family is roaming around the grounds with their spray-tanned skin and overdressed children and Teresa's husband says something seriously offensive about autism. When your parents die, another character remarks, all you have left are your siblings. I'm briefly touched. Later, someone throws a half-hearted punch at someone else and a third person calls: "It's like speaking to a wall . . . !!" in the direction of nothing else.

•

One of the first times we spoke I guessed nine out of ten of his "top influences" (I skipped Marianne Moore—he didn't look old enough). It's not difficult to pick up on the trends. When I lived here the first time Surrealism was all the rage, or at least a type of poetics rife with non sequitur, deadpan, shape-shifting, and irony. In those years we were thrilled by Roberto Bolaño, Sei Shōnagon, *Lost*, writers named Matt or Mark or Kyle or Zach, whiskey, western shirts, jokes. Students the following year adored Jack Spicer, Theresa Hak Kyung Cha, weed, and sleeping in. Recently the writers seem committed to an

Ivy League education, painkillers, Jean-Michel Basquiat, Sara Ahmed, and robots. Some things never go out of style. One week I walked into the Foxhead and overnight all of the guys had acquired frayed tank tops and ratty, fratty baseball caps. It was a case of *abro*priation. This is my life but this isn't all of it.

.

(Michelle Kehoe and her children, sailing through the sky; what a strange sight that must have been for someone driving by . . . )

.

It was a Wednesday night at George's. The regulars were competing via jukebox (Bill Withers preceding Drake, Joy Division trailing Smog), and although most of the faces I saw were swollen, we were each faithfully present that evening, we were all *loyally there* to pretend someone else wasn't. We were harvesting the wreckage of wild fun. M. told us of the recent dearth in a long tradition of Korean female divers while, out of the corners of our eyes, we watched who walked in, who walked out, who sat down next to whom and in which booth. At a certain point I stood up and J. grabbed my ass. It was okay; it was his birthday. A. pushed J.'s hand away. J. smiled widely and slapped A. hard across the face. Then the scene, from the very beginning, repeated itself. Once, I pitched the idea of a complimentary periscope arriving with each drink, a tool with which to better spy on other booths. Another time we invented a touch-screen table from which one could access documents pertaining to the person being talked about. We floated the

idea, too, of adding a lobby managed by forties-era hostesses—
red lipstick, lined nylons, pin curls—who would deliver a rotary
phone to the table for communication with out-of-towners or
hearsay on behalf of those at home. It turned out there was a
lot to think about while posing patiently in plain sight, helping
your designated ignorer ignore you.

•

Games We Play: Cracker, Lime, or Nothing; M v. W; The Fake
Goodbye; Cannoli / Pepperoni; Bags; Beads, Beads, Beads!; In-
side or Outside?; Small or Far Away?; The All Crawl; Euchre;
The Podcast; P.O. __; Team Babes; Act Natural; You Put Me in
a Situation; *The West Wing* Whistle; What's More Similar; In
Racine; Soft Gs; The Deepest V; You Dropped a Dot; BOGO
Package (3/12 to 3/15); Old Man Dance; Egyptian Rat Fuck;
Better One . . . Better Two?; Face Swap; Option Man; Little
Women; See You in Hell; Boop!; The Years and Hours of Em-
ily Dickinson.

•

Pink and red wash . . . copper scribble of a passed-out drunk.
Faint green pressing up from the lower left-hand corner.
Hair-thin charcoal scratches in soft gray light to the right.
Pronounced, perfect bourbon bottles rendered in oil . . . pen-
cil lines . . . canvas grain. I click on more links. I am watching young men throw boiling pots of water into the air. Some
stand on a patio, some in the yard, and one leans over what
appears to be a ten-story balcony in eastern Russia. Water
flies into the ether and—due to scientific principles I don't

understand—instantaneously morphs into smoke. A thick and cottony frozen cloud; a billowing snow wall. We're living in a "polar vortex" and are waiting it out inside, safe from nature. In Hendrick Avercamp's *Winter Landscape with Ice Skaters* an entire town drifts aimlessly across an icy field. Yesterday morning at the corner of Gilbert and Davenport I slid for an instant on the sidewalk and nearly split open my skull. No one saw. I examine the backs of two children perched on a boat in the foreground. There's a skater dressed in a fool's yellow hat and matching pantaloons. Crows peck at the corpse of a frozen horse. When I saw this painting for the first time, many years ago, in the dim light of an art museum in Amsterdam, I swore to myself that I'd never forget it. I did though, for two years, and then I remembered.

∙

Winter sun seeps through the snow on the angled panes of the farmhouse. "What's so funny?" *Mmmm. Mmmmhmmmm.* A drowsy wiggle. "What are you laughing at?" "The fruit," he responds from some remote interior location, some distant foreign dream that I will never reach. "The fruit" . . . more laughter . . . a deeper sleep . . . "There are just so many . . . different . . . types of . . . *fruit.*"

∙

S. unfolds a midsized cardboard flat from the twined bulk batch propped against the reception desk, pops open the segments, and turns down four rectangular panels in quick succession. He bends each tan appendage so that the two longer exterior edges match in the middle and slides packing tape across the ensuing gap—twice—for extra strength. I try to lesser effect: the joints where the sides meet are still attached. The tape repeatedly rips midswing and I cut my thumb—*a thrill!*—with the serrated edges of the tape gun. The dean demands that our office move. It's political and out of my purview. Once the boxes are formed, I'm an expert. I fit rectangles in with like rectangles, small boxes of staples or paper clips along the edges, and I can swiftly identify which ancient furniture is bound for donation. Last week, A. spoke at length with the night custodian in the basement. He wants to be a writer. Little does he know that we must now close our imaginations to the places we inhabit. Say goodbye to familiar ghosts!

•

The chief sentiment is shame. Shame and secrets; secret shame. An all-purpose excuse and punishment; both accurate and self-indulgent; a terrifying purgatory, a weather vane. So-and-so won't speak to so-and-so because she betrayed him; she broke his heart. Now no one can be in the same room. But, oh, don't blame so-and-so for abandoning you outside a locked house, he was messed up, he *can't recall.* Please forgive so-and-so for acting brisk and distant, he's prone to anxiety and distrust. Don't expect too much of so-and-so, she doesn't know what she's doing, she *feels bad.* The shame, he says, has *shut him down.* It's hard not to feel that the point's been missed. Amidst the confusion, the humiliation, the angst, and disease, the bodies in this town will still march several times a week toward H., steady H., and she will deliver unto legions one Jameson on the rocks with a Guinness back. A soldier of the plains, a Viking queen, we'd follow her to the ends of the earth; we'd enlist. *Nurse*, wrote our only knowing predecessor, the one who couldn't save us.

•

It becomes harder and harder to leave the house. Shards are evidence. The shovel's missing and there is no salt. No one need believe this.

•

That girl's a bore. A total drag. At first I didn't think—with her frantic manic anecdotes, her frenzied center-of-this-coffee-shop laugh—that she knew. But she knows. I am irritated by my own sad malice. Those gestures, those dirty hipster eighties glasses, that cloying tone—it comes from a desperation I hope that I never know. The interesting thing about the girl being such a bore is not that she *is* a bore but that she has the *exact same name* and *exact same haircut* and *exact same tedious affect* as the biggest bore in town the last time I lived here. So, in some ways, although she is a bore, by being an exact replica of another bore she is additionally astonishing. It seems impossible that there could exist so many similar versions, so much meanness (me), and the perpetual cliché of an insipid pretentious cackling young being. An abandoned cruise ship filled with cannibal rats drifts unmanned through the high seas. What is this news.

•

Chris Kraus wrote that "empathy is not a reaching outward. It is a loop. Because there isn't any separation anymore between what you are and what you see." I fold the white wax paper around my burger. I pick at the cheese. One time I saw a film reel burst into slow flames—a black rainbow—through the projection of itself on the screen.

•

They laughed so hard they cried. They almost died. They were hilariously "in love." They broke up. It took the better part of an hour to find the woman's used blue VW Rabbit at the Coralville mall, both of them having forgotten where they'd parked it. The man told the story—one she'd heard several times—of how his grandfather, adrift in a dangerous Colorado blizzard, survived by chewing on thin slices of the elk he'd shot at the start of the whiteout. In the mall the woman had tried on a gold dress made of glitter. The man bought two shirts. "This wasn't a good place to be," wrote Leonard Michaels in his diaries, "but I couldn't leave."

•

I turn on the television. I see an adult man watching television. An adult woman is watching the adult man watch television. She asks: *Is there anything that you want? Is there anything that I can get you?* He doesn't respond. I came here in a charitable mood. I turn it off.

•

Once my brother P. was riding the El to work when a man, he noticed, was watching him from a seat across the way. P. returned to his book. When he looked up again he caught the eye of the watcher, still watching. This time P. realized that the man, this watcher, was someone he had gone to high school with several years ago in a suburb of Chicago. They had been neither friends nor enemies. When P.'s stop grew near he stood and walked across the jostling train in the direction of the sliding doors. The man turned his face to P. and performed a look—one we've all seen—of elated, animated recognition; "P.!," he exclaimed, "P.!—it's *so* good to see you!" P. met his eyes and smiled. "No," he replied, hopping onto the wooden platform, "I'm sorry, but you must be mistaken."

•

Chicken with lemon, onion, garlic, sriracha, mustard, salt, pepper, oil, burnt. Add avocado, apple, almonds, goat cheese, any fruit, vegetables, lettuce, herbs.

•

I want to understand more than I do. You should too. I walk to the library and leaf through books on dependency, mood disorders, drug abuse. I research pathological behavior and depression, rehab, and the neurological links between art and madness. There's proof enough. I can't tell you how to get better. I can't help you more than I tried. You nearly died. That summer, after returning from visiting you in the hospital, from calling doctors and your mother, delivering a toothbrush and a change of clothes, A. would sit across from me and listen. She would order a crème de menthe and Sprite, then lean across the table, like an angel, and say what was already always those days on my mind. What she said was true. Perhaps it was clearer to everyone else, but I knew: at every moment that it mattered, you lied.

.

K. finds a key in the rock. D. throws a butterfly knife through the crowd of drunken dancers. L. pops E.'s blow-up giraffe hat. Someone barfs in the garden. M. dons drinking-straw glasses filled with wine and performs a series of Ella Fitzgerald songs. A. makes mimosas for the shower. We got ourselves into this mess, that's for sure. We're the only ones to blame. Day after day it's the same. A few of us have jobs, no money. Some sleep past noon! One day I am thinking of a young Martin Sheen dashing with high knees through the woodlands, cradling a shotgun against his bare chest, while Sissy Spacek, all freckles and calm, waits for him in a tree house. They've recently murdered. The famous poet is sitting next to me while we watch a famous novelist read. Afterwards, I am introduced to everyone. We walk to the bar and a large group of glow-in-the-dark skull-masked strangers jump out at me from the shadows. "Surprise!!," they scream.

# Out of Nowhere Into Nothing

In March 1941, Sherwood Anderson, sixty-four at the time, could be found aboard a cruise ship to South America with his fourth wife, Eleanor Gladys Copenhaver, when he knocked back a martini whose olive's toothpick would, over the course of the night, make its way almost completely through the internal piping of his throat, stomach, and intestines before—in the so-called *homestretch*—puncturing his colon and sending him into a fevered shock of infection and inflammation (later diagnosed as peritonitis) that would—two days later in a military hospital located in the aptly named Colón, Panama—kill him, or so I think I remember correctly from a poorly made reenactment of the event on late night cable in the basement of D.'s parents' house in West Des Moines one summer over a decade ago. The program was called something like *The Dramatic Deaths of Celebrities* or *How Famous People Pass*, and when

I search for it now I find no evidence of its existence, though I could never forget the CGI graphic of a slim slow-motion stick—a pointed cocktail prop—sailing through the poorly drawn canals of what was supposed to represent the inside of—everyone's? anyone's?—intestines as it slid awkwardly around the body's bends like a panicked child down a waterslide. At the time I had read only the most popular of Anderson's works—*Winesburg, Ohio*—and had yet to familiarize myself with his more obscure stories or underrated and remarkable poetry (to Eleanor he once wrote "I really want only to write poetry but do not want to be called a poet. To be known as a poet is rather too much like being known as a lover."); I had yet to reside in the city he was from (Cleveland), value accessorized liquor, or discover Anderson's ongoing correspondence with Gertrude Stein, although I did know of Stein's connection to William James (she had been a student of his in the Harvard Psychology Department), adding to the ongoing series of associations among writers that at first might appear coincidental but upon reflection is inevitable and perhaps even obvious. I recognized Anderson as a B-list early twentieth-century writer (he was in fact a major inspiration to Hemingway and Faulkner, both of whom he published), but when one summer in the stacks of a used bookstore in Chicago I stumbled across the story "War," from his 1921 collection *The Triumph of the Egg*, something in the way the tale was told wholly stunned me. The four-page story begins with the narrator on a midnight train rushing through bleak Midwestern prairieland, just one passenger among a crowded train of nameless strangers waiting in a drowsy daze to arrive at their undisclosed location. Our narrator makes quite clear that the story he is telling simply *occurred*, the story that would stick with him in such a way that he was compelled to forever share it had *just arrived*; it arrived unasked for from a woman on a train who, as if in a trance, delivered it to him, a fortunate stranger, for no reason other than his presence. The woman started her story (we were midway through ours) by telling the stranger that she had been to war. She is described as having come from war-ridden Poland and is perhaps, though not clearly, traveling with a man dressed in a dark brown cloak who is throughout the occasion of the exchange hovering—pacing the hall of the train, trying to reclaim his seat—witnessed by the narrator but not recognized as the woman's lover until the events of the evening are reflected upon for the sake of retelling. The woman explained how on a dark and windy winter evening a group of Polish refugees were directed by a German officer across the border. They were tired and hungry and worn, and the officer kept them marching at a brisk pace along the side of the rural road toward what was unquestionably more violence. At a certain point, so Anderson's narrator's acquaintance's story goes, an exhausted elderly woman and the officer began to fight, physically though weakly, and the train mate describes the strangeness of this struggle for quite some time before concluding her tale with the succinct scene of an actual *battle of the souls* in which the essence of the old woman transcends her physical body and enters the body of the German and the essence of the German in turn enters the old woman and the body of the woman then recommands the crowd of captives and commences marching them in the direction of their doom again. "Their two souls began to struggle," says Anderson's narrator; "the woman in the train made me understand that quite clearly, although it may be difficult to get the sense of it over to you. I had the night and the mystery of the moving train to help me . . ." It is impossible in this moment for one not to feel within their rotting reader's body the rushing mystical bewildering mystery of that fated evening (can't you just *smell* the smoky train car now? can't you feel the freeze of the window on your cheek as the bleak Nebraska fields fly by, unseen but still *perceived by you?*), a feeling which is in part provoked by Anderson's narrator's nonchalant but insisted distance—for who among us doesn't fight more fiercely to grasp what they're told is impossible to comprehend!? By simply denying his listener's imaginative potential— in a seemingly offhand comment—Anderson's narrator increases our attention to the existence of the blazing train, to the woman's report, and to the possibility of our own old souls someday magically switching places with their enemy. It is perhaps because of his pointed point-of-view maneuverings and multilayered frames (like Dickinson's endlessly breaking Plank in Reason, "War" splits open each beginning to reveal another tier in the tale) that Anderson is considered a "psychological" writer; he becomes, midcareer, preoccupied with telling you, the reader, *why* the narrator is telling you what the narrator is telling you—of making an argument for the import of a story well conveyed, honorably illustrated; crowded with faults, errors, hearsay, and gossip; of fictionalized versions of fiction— and yet critics have described his stories as "moving but formless," the action hypothesized as haphazard and disorienting even to Anderson while inventing it. It's true: repeatedly in Anderson's work a speaker will confess his confusion, his bewilderment not only with the predicament at hand but, upon reflection, *the very meaning* of the situation he is bound to divulge, much as one might process or "work through" a traumatic memory in therapy. Anderson's narrators document the "facts" (of the fiction) "objectively" while almost reluctantly including an editorial view that is purely subjective; for example, the young male narrator in "Death in the Woods" insists that while the story at hand—about a death in the woods—was communicated accurately to the town, it was not *expressed* properly, and not only that, he explains, but in his opinion no one who was present at the time really understood the significance of the events as they had unfolded. "The fragments," he says, "had to be picked up slowly, long afterwards." What surfaces is the tension of disclosure rather than the consequences of the action as it happens. It is this tension that recalls me to something my friend L. once read about how emotions only exist in the body for a minute and a half, and it's our own impulse to account for them that permits sentiment any sustaining power, so that ultimately our feelings are stories. I found whole theories born of the "ninety-second rule," each claiming that mere seconds pass from the moment an emotion is triggered to the moment it exits the bloodstream (if, for example, you are furious, you might try counting to ninety, one website suggests, and chances are your rage will fade), although one cannot help but fret about the equal brevity of love or delight, as those feelings too must slip so swiftly through the body. William James posited the now-outdated theory that our emotions are actually *caused* by physiological activity in a specific context, that what we commonly refer to as an "emotion" is the brain recognizing and responding to corporeal information. If we were to consider, for example, the case of a woman who, late one February night was being driven by her then-boyfriend G.

toward the downtown of a small college town and, hypothetically, when they pulled up to a stop sign he threw open the driver's side door, leapt suddenly out of the vehicle and hit the ground running toward a group of frightened sophomore-looking bros—one of whom was passed out, slowly slipping from the back of an open SUV, overdosing, dripping like putty, his skull about to slam into frozen concrete—and within minutes, say, the cops arrived and instructed the woman not to leave, not to go anywhere, and in the resulting confusion of alarms and screams ("He's not breathing! He's not breathing!") everyone else on the scene, including G., was arrested and rushed away, leaving the woman alone on a street knowing that everything was terribly wrong, then, in that moment, we would know the woman would find her heart racing, palms hot, eyes blurring because—according to James's theory—the brain's reaction to that physical state (which was caused by its *environment*) is what one calls "fear," and furthermore might only exist in the body in less-than-two-minute increments. "Can one fancy the state of rage and picture no ebullition of it in the chest?," James asks in "What Is an Emotion?;" "no flushing of the face, no dilatation of the nostrils, no clenching of the teeth, no impulse to vigorous action, but in their stead limp muscles, calm breathing, and a placid face?" And are we then *forced* to feel these passions via the alchemy of art? In an essay by Lee Ann Roripaugh, first sent to me by E., I learned that mirror neurons—involved in empathy, pain, and language—supposedly make it possible not only to physically *feel* the experience of another while witnessing their action, but to also feel an echo of what they feel when we read about it. Roripaugh quotes one of the discoverers of the mirror neuron, Dr. Giacomo Rizzolatti, who explains that "Mirror neurons allow us to grasp the minds of others not through conceptual reasoning but through direct simulation. By feeling not by thinking," so that, for example, as Catherine dies I know the grief of Heathcliff, or when James Wright has claimed to have wasted his life, so too have I, and when Anderson explains the mystery of the rushing train my mirror neurons fire, and when I describe the mystery of the rushing train to you, you feel it too. One cannot help but wonder whether emotion in art is desirable—either to have *or* to cause—and if there's much of a choice. It was just last week that my class and I were discussing the various ambiguities of so-called "reality" in art when I brought up the scene from the third season of the American show *The Office* where Jim leans around the doorframe into a room where his longtime crush Pam is talking to a "documentary" filmmaker in order to ask her out. A moment later the actress who plays Pam, Jenna Fischer, turns her head back to the camera and smiles, blushes, grins, looks down, then up, her eyes watering in absolute joy. It is a poignant nonverbal (if sentimental) instant that conveys the cyclone of emotions love provokes. And yet, according to an interview—was it with Terry Gross?—Fischer was not merely acting: in the split second after she turned her head back to the camera she looked into the eyes of the true *and* fictional (unseen) cameraman who, in real life and in real time, responded to the storyline—the drama of a long-awaited relationship—by tearing up and, although his involuntary reaction to the story occurred off camera, Fischer (still being filmed as Pam) saw the cameraman cry and, therefore, cried too. And so did I, I tell them, and so would you. Do we turn to art for catharsis? What is an emotion's rate of decay? I will say only that

I haven't stopped feeling for a fictional old woman and have thought about little else since.

# Wild America

M. and I were haunting Basta's happy hour—half-priced drinks—for the third time that week. It was early June, unusually hot, and we goofed and gossiped all afternoon beneath the burn of the swollen sun. It was the summer preceding Obama's reelection, and we were sipping our second sweating carafe of cheap white wine from the perch of Basta's raised porch, surveying small herds of soggy strangers stroll down Iowa Ave., when M. pursued the loose thread of our conversation into a story about a college friend's childhood vision of her brother's near-death experience. This was not unusual subject matter for us and M. slid quickly into the tale, accustomed as we were to swapping fragmented recollections of coincidence and the uncanny. When she spoke, M.'s earrings—dangling chartreuse orbs crowned with specks of diamond—made small, almost imperceptible circles to the sides of her mouth; two unripe royal suns in permanent tremor. As a girl, M. had harbored a crush on her friend's younger brother, a boy of hazelnut hair and syrupy eyes, and this perhaps, she suggested, enhanced the vibrant and tender manner of her narration. Apparently, when M.'s college friend was quite young, maybe five, she awoke one evening from a nightmare screaming at the top of her lungs and raced into her parents' bedroom in a paranoid panic. Once in the safety of her mother's arms she reported having seen in her sleep a peculiar formation the size of a baseball lying dormant in her little brother's forehead and with tiny digits she circled the location on her own head where she believed the mass to exist in her sibling. The girl wept furiously; she insisted that what she had seen in her dream was accurate. Her parents, as anyone's parents would, put the girl back to bed, more amused than worried. Also, M. said, the dream contained a scene in which the mysterious growth oozed through the brother's brain through his nostrils. M. had worked in medicine, surgery specifically, before becoming the poet and scholar I knew her as, and she was the only human I'd ever met who once held a still-beating heart in the cupped hollows of her calm palms. The idea of cradling a living heart was both magnificent and unfathomable and each time she repeated it—often at my urging—I felt awesomely alien from what I understood of mortality. M.'s familiarity with the technical internal machinations of the body couldn't help but lend a noteworthy weight to any story of psychic or near-death experience and in part I reveled in her accounts because they revealed clues to the clinical life she inhabited before we met in Iowa City, the quiet college town where I returned for work every summer and where she had lived for over eight years. We shifted in Basta's wire chairs as the waiter brought out our olives, the wine glasses sliding through puddles of condensation on the top of the table. M. explained how decades later her college friend's brother was diagnosed with a terminal brain tumor. His cancer was discovered in the precise spot his sister had predicted so many years ago and upon closer diagnoses it even proved to occupy *the exact dimensions and character* she had described as a child. Her brother consequently participated in several treatments—radiation, chemo—and after months of discouraging results his doctors suggested a somewhat risky final surgery that would involve removing the tumor by drawing it down through his sinuses. This was, M. said, taking a sip of ice water, when her friend knew he would survive it. For several years I had been interested in narratives like these, narratives that demonstrated transformative foresight, concentrated coincidence, psychic skirmish. This ·interest had grown so obsessive that I felt responsible for every innocuous conversation's turn toward testimonies of the impossible. Because of the nature of my seasonal work—administration for a summer writing program—this was the time of year I found myself the most social and it became a dinner party habit to interview friends and colleagues about events that occurred outside the customary limits of logic. It seemed as if everyone I spoke with had at least one story, one little tale, no matter how tangential or potentially ordinary, that fell into the category of the so-called *paranormal.* Some friends believed these stories contained evidence of a universe unknown, fraught with psychological or religious implications. Some thought the subject nonsense but reveled in disclosing their account regardless. I was mostly interested in the narratives as they related to a set of specific historical

experiments I was studying; for several years I had been preoccupied with the transcripts, tests, and texts of the late 1800s
scientific association the Society for Psychical Research. On
my walk home from Basta that evening—through the ped mall
and a mile or so down College Street—I thought of a story I'd
once read about Henry and William James, both of whom
were infamously interested in the apparitional. William—the
more avidly invested in the paranormal of the two and a found-
ing member of the SPR—asked both Henry and Alice (William's wife) to attempt communication with him after he died
or at least to permit his post-death psychic advances. In order
to guarantee that William's ghost would be recognizable they
all agreed upon a code word that would unmistakably identify
his soul as the one trying to get in touch. In all likelihood Henry, who was fascinated with the fictional possibilities of the occult but not necessarily their reality, was annoyed. From what I
recall of the story, Henry and Alice obediently entertained a
single medium after William's death and when no contact was
made they gave up. When telling this story to others, I always
catch myself claiming the word *pineapple* as the psychic trig-
gering term and I wonder now if this is an accurate tidbit of the
original anecdote or a detail lazily inserted into an already blur-
ry history, a bogus repetition irreverently invented altogether.
Once I spent a few afternoons searching for a source that
would confirm the word *pineapple* as the key to James's ghost
and instead discovered an article discussing a similar pact between William James and Frederic Myers, his partner in the
SPR and the man who coined the term "telepathy." The article
described how James stationed himself in a chair outside the
bedroom in Rome where, in 1901, Myers was dying. James was

too scared to enter, too upset to witness his good friend's death, but wanted to honor his promise to receive any psychic message shot in his direction. James's notebook, according to records, remained empty. Nonetheless, the idea of an agreed-upon phrase acting as the hinge between life and death remained to the SPR, and to myself, profoundly moving. James later wrote in a memorial for Myers that there were two practiced approaches to psychology at the time, the "classic academic" and the "romantic" type. The first method was extremely efficient, rigorous, and "intolerant of either nondescript facts or clumsy formulas"; all data was controlled through precise classifications and new developments were expected to fit into approved scientific systems. The second type, the "romantic" type, for which Myers was credited as a practitioner, was chaotic, creative, imaginative, and volatile. James continued in this homage to his friend (which initially appeared in the pages of the *Proceedings of the Society for Psychical Research*) to claim that recent psychology had been replete with romantic thinkers and to encounter their work was "like going from classic to Gothic architecture, where few outlines are pure and where uncouth forms lurk in the shadows." Even if the connection between souls could not be wholly confirmed I imagined James and Myers hoping that a simple code could provoke an echo from the dead to the living. The concept of a telepathic password, although likely impossible, seemed an inventive method of approaching the potential existence of the spirit in a measured (if literary) manner. One thinks not only of those words fraught with physical or historically traumatic definitions: *slut*, *God*, *fetus*, etc.—but of common, seemingly trivial words that through repeated annunciation can trouble comprehension.

For example, I was once emailed a link to one of the artist Steve Snell's videos, in which Snell experiments with repetition by creating adventure art from media depicting outdoor exploration. In the piece, made in 2009, the kitschy D-list celebrity Marty Stouffer—whom one might recall as the sandy-bearded crimson-faced host of the 1980s PBS wildlife adventure show *Wild America* (later controversial for rumors concerning staged animal violence and "fictional" wildlife scenes)—appears on the screen manically introducing himself, as he did at the start of every episode, with the phrase "I'm Marty Stouffer!" over and over again in one- to four-second clips extracted from what must be at least 100 shows, the video lasting about five and a half minutes total. In each clip in Snell's video Stouffer is grinning outrageously at the camera or striking a conspicuously faux unfussy pose while he leans against the peeling bark of a birch or hunches on his accomplished haunches near a babbling brook. In each clip Stouffer dons (or is donned with?) a ridiculous striped woolen sweater or western flannel button-up. In some cuts Stouffer interacts with a curious dog, child, or bluebird. He is often, though not always, outdoors—occasionally instead resting on a weathered leather chair or in front of an instructional drawing of a brown bear or trout. In about half of the clips he wears a pair of binoculars around his neck like a doctor flashing a stethoscope as evidence of competence. One notices these differences because the video is quite simply Marty Stouffer—eternal, unrelenting Marty Stouffer—announcing himself repeatedly—*I'm Marty Stouffer!*, *I'm Marty Stouffer!*, *I'm Marty Stouffer!*, *I'm Marty Stouffer!*— in a seemingly endless—enthusiastic, hellish—introduction. The Snell video proceeds in such a way as to make one feel instantaneously and hysterically insane, as if you (or I?) were (and forever are?) transforming into the very identity and person of this *alleged* Marty Stouffer (let's all say it together now!: *I'm Marty Stouffer!*, *I'm Marty Stouffer!* . . . ), slowly dissolving into his voice, liquefying into the ether, each molecule of your body *becoming* these five syllables, these three words, until one's own face is not their face, one's name is not their name, one's brain can only remain intact if inhabiting the form of Stouffer's (Snell-curated) chanting (the chanting now your chanting, the rhythm now your rhythm, the words just sounds that surge and blur past meaning: *iyemarteestaughwffffer*) as you are always and forever more a little bit of Marty, spellbound, entranced, trapped inside this video, this (Stouffer's? Snell's?) consciousness, gazing right now—*now*, from inside—back out through the blazing screen, through the reflection of your own old mug at the pre-Stouffer soul in the process of surrendering to an existence already exhausted by a back-lit box. I will not pretend to recall the exact instant that Marty Stouffer's voice imprisoned me, nor can I say for certain that every viewer would respond in a similar fashion, but I can testify that this severance of self occurred each time I was drawn to (*why?*—you might ask—*why?*) press play on the digital video. If repetition kills anticipation, it also halts time (the time it takes to expect change), and I wondered, on the walk home from drinks with M., about this trance-like sensation, the levitation of one word or phrase repeated, the same pattern elongated, as occurs in prayer, hex, (madness?), or meditation. The video inspired the sudden possibility, though difficult to express, that one might learn to leave the structure of time behind, to unmoor the self from the singular present in order to exist in an associative, multiplane, synchronized state that could somehow carry a crowd of conduits. The sensation was dizzying, abstract, pleasurable, demented—and, like so many human flashes of insight, it was indescribable, impractical, fleeting, absurd, and felt more brutally precise than the truths that plague and govern average daily reasoning. One discovers that these sudden sparks of clarity arise from the bleak and tedious muck of the mind rarely, and when they do they depart just as quickly as they flared: ripple-fearing minnows in a stone-thrown pond. It is the swift conviction of unearned knowledge that lends one such a cruel hope. I could not have known it at the time, but a few days after the evening's walk home from Basta, I would have a conversation with my friend V. in which he explained that as a child he often repeated the same word over and over again to himself in order to combat the raging army of shadows that marched along his bedroom walls while he struggled to sleep. The word that looped through his mind as defense was his own name, *V.*, and he would take comfort in this charm, this self-sung lullaby, the chant alienating his mind from his body, actualizing the calm he required to separate, however briefly, from his own overwhelming consciousness. Later, when investigating obsessive repetition, sometimes associated with lunacy or paranoia, I found that the occurrence, "semantic sensation" (or "semantic saturation"), happens when the reiteration of a single word or phrase invokes the uncanny feeling that it has abandoned its meaning. The neurological effect is similar to *jamais vu*, a circumstance in which repetition summons disbelief in a word's purpose or when one doubts one's ability to understand language, to comprehend connotation. I cannot help but to think of Melville's Bartleby, who through the insistence of his one sure phrase, *I would prefer not to*, is so famous for having shifted the moral and ethical emotional landscape of the fictional office in which he worked. Bartleby's echo does not correspond exactly with the symptoms of semantic sensation but is perhaps a slowed-down version that similarly calls into question the myriad of ways in which a single phrase may collapse understanding, gradually destroying reference and stealing new strength from the hollow vacancy of recurring sound. Bartleby's mantra is a mirror to all who hear it, a noise for one to react through, and an example of the form of a phrase impeccably actualizing the content it wishes to evoke— inspiring further discomfort in its recipients; extreme apathy and denial in the speaker (as the coldness of repetition does)— with irony manifesting in the fact that replication undoes the listener's literal experience, making the declaration (of indifference) appropriately dull and foreign. The names of things are what make them stick, we'd like to think, until they circle unrelentingly, and then, like an old Victorian parlor trick, the mind rises through the brain and floats from its home in the head, disengaging one's so-called *grounded* personality from command. V., as a young boy falling asleep, could no longer maintain faith in the fact that the word he whispered to himself—his name—was a sound that indicated identity. Nor could he accept that it signified *anything*: after all, that was the point of the exercise. It is strange that at such a young age humans are able to—or desire to—disassociate the mind from the body as a mode of relief or survival, repetition forcing a ghost of the waking brain. Perhaps language that connects the living to the dead is as likely to exist as those terms that sever the inside from out, so that one is, in a way, speaking to one's own self dead, each time there is a psychic divide. That night, as I continued down College Street, I rolled a random word through my mind hoping for a telepathic connection: *bunker, bunker, bunker, bunker, bunker, bunker, bunker, bunker, bunker, bunker, bunker, bunker, bunker, bunker, bunker, bunker, bunker, bunker, bunker, bunker, bunker, bunker, bunker, bunker, bunker, bunker, bunker, bunker, bunker, bunker, bunker, bunker, bunker, bunker, bunker*......... nothing. The word crumbled; *bunker* at first the cave under a house and then two onerous beats of static. At that point in the evening the sinking sun hung so red that I had to squint while crossing Governor, and as I neared my temporary home for the summer I noticed the scorched straw lawns that lined the lane and a pitiable bubble of creek flow. The streets stretched vacant, blank, devoid of children. The trees stood still. Three months from then I would no longer reside in Iowa—I was just *passing through*—but each instance thereafter I encountered the word *bunker* I would find myself abruptly transported to the corner of College and Muscatine as well as the consciousness I inhabited that June. A bat shot by. Crickets scraped their shanks in the arid shade. *Basta, baseball, chaos, wine; absence, cancer, shadows.* The possibilities swung high and wide—they sailed into whispering phone lines and jumbled until one of them stuck. That night I received a word that will splinter ether in order to transmit. Later, I'll affirm what I heard. I'll confess to you the sounds one can expect me to toss from the coffin.

# Driving at Night: A Chorus

The thin, circular flap flips back. No thicker than a sliver of thread. It's slid out and set aside, still attached, the opening of a porthole on its hinge. Recognize—somehow, and for the first time—the smell of your own eyeball burning as you watch the top of it removed. Sliced right off. Your cornea is left tethered to the eye by just a single small string. "The cornea is . . . peeled back and the underlying cornea tissue is reshaped using an excimer laser."

"After the cornea is reshaped so that it can properly focus light into the eye and onto the retina, [the] flap is put back. . . ." A transparent, deflated balloon. You're drugged and bleary, the blurred lullaby of surgery. Lashes are taped to their brows, lids held open. It is impossible to shift as you witness your own voluntary blindness. It comes upon you as a circle of absolute darkness encroaching upon a crescent of florescent light. Solar eclipse, a covered urn, the replacing of a lens cap after the photographer has left the room.

*July, 1882.*
*I was expecting my husband home, and shortly after the time he ought to have arrived (about 10 p.m.) I heard a cab drive up to the door, the bell ring, my husband's voice talking with the cabman, the front door open, and his step come up the stairs. I went to the drawing room, opened it, and to my astonishment saw no one. I could hardly believe he was not there, the whole thing was so vivid, and the street was particularly quiet at the time. About 20 minutes or so after this my husband really arrived, though nothing sounded to me more real than it did the first time. The train was late, and he had been thinking I might be anxious.*
*Amy C. Powys*

Some nights there is an occasion for travel after dusk—either for pleasure or interest, delivering an item, or god forbid an emergency. The swollen night sky voids from view shapes or traces of matter padding narrow—transient, circular—units of space in space in space still spiraling. Missing or damaged cones prevent you from steering straight or knowing where the edge lies. Orange cones can separate lanes; others divide the eye. "For there are some errors that are caused in all the senses and others that are confined to things seen, of which some are visual and others are in the mind." *I saw a man dart across the road—I hit the brakes. There was no man, just space. Honking cars behind me.*

If faith was enough, we would not need to see something in order to believe (in) it. But it is difficult not to believe in the actual shapes that we do see. What it means to hallucinate remains a question. Common usage suggests an uncontrolled, outside-one's-self, freestanding visual image. Like a hologram from an unidentified source, or a kaleidoscope of sorts—pulling material from some hidden organization of light, color, and reflection. Too, the sensation might include unrecognized or untraceable voices. Phantom limbs, false instincts, levitation.

*Formication* is the feeling of insects crawling all over one's body and *phantosmia* is when you smell an odor that doesn't exist. Hallucinations are "distinguished from *illusion* in the strict sense as not necessarily involving a false belief." Not purposeful deceit, manufactured trickery, or mere sense-driven diversion. *Hallucination* is the name for a perception of something that *is not there*, that *does not exist*, or *has not occurred* within our material and tangible world. Like dark matter, dreams, hypotheses, ideas: lacking in matter. Visual hallucinations, or apparitions, "may be called 'objective' facts, although they are not 'material' facts"—an experience unexperienced, a false happening, a nonoccurrence, strife. But a hallucination is physical, it does take time, it still contributes to the compost of a life.

Much of the most innovative early research into the occurrence of hallucinations was documented by the Society for Psychical Research. Comprised of some of the more creative scholars of the late 1800s—William James, Henry and Eleanor Sidgwick,

Frederic W. H. Myers, Edmund Gurney—the SPR investigated paranormal, psychical, mediumistic, and ghostly phenomenon. They were a democratic, collaborative, and somewhat international community intent on gathering exact testimonies from the public at large. They were also interested in following all mysterious leads, assessing objective facts, and narrowing in on the kinds of questions science might ask of the unknown. The SPR endeavored to explore what it didn't already understand about medicine, the human mind, coincidence, instincts, telepathy, hypnosis, and what connections might exist between thinking minds and human bodies after death. An exploration or explosion of facts. An "investigation, [or] inquiry into things."

*February 7th, 1884.*
*While a resident of the city of Philadelphia, I made an appointment to meet a personal friend. At the appointed hour I was at the designated place. My friend was tardy in his appearing. After a while, however, I saw him approaching (or thought I did). So assured was I of his advance that I advanced to meet him, when presently he disappeared entirely.*

*The locality where I thought I saw his approach was open, and unobstructed by any object behind which he could have disappeared. Only by leaping a high brick wall (an enclosure of a burying-ground) could he have secreted himself. The hallucination was complete—so distinct as to lead me to advance to meet him without a thought of optical illusion.*

*I immediately went to the office of my friend, and there learned from him that he had not been away from his desk for several hours.*

*The appointment was forgotten by my friend, as he stated in his apology when I entered his office.*
*F. R. Harbaugh*


One always sees an object at a distance. There is space between the self and what is perceived—a length of time dividing. To see is to expect the past. To permit or capture what once stood in front of you or acknowledge what has already absented. The time it takes for an eye to process an image is infinitesimal. It is the speed of light and can feel like a forecasting current.


Stripped of sight, in surgery, you think of this. With utmost concentration you conjure a presence as if in prayer. Envision the doctor hovering over you. He focuses the laser on the precise horizon that forms the ring of the iris. Imagined scenes always occur like this: slow-motion mental pictures. As a film that projects by the light of your mind, it can unwind. The white room can occur at will, without vision or awareness of time.


In *Phantasms of the Living*, Edmund Gurney (the first secretary of the SPR), along with Frank Podmore and Frederic Myers, organized an extensive compilation of firsthand accounts portraying "hallucinations of the sane," flukes, hauntings, and hypnotism. Published in 1886, the two volumes of *Phantasms of the Living* contained 702 cases of confirmed psychical events. Based on the gathered material, Gurney, Podmore, and Myers hypothesized that crisis apparitions (wherein a person sees or hears an apparition at the approximate time in which the living physical body of that apparition, elsewhere, is experiencing an emergency, crisis, or death) are hallucinations in the mind of the viewer and are caused by telepathic messages sent by the body that is dying or experiencing trauma. "Gurney's explanation [was] that the mind of the person undergoing the calamity was at that moment able to impress the mind of the percipient with [a] hallucination." Not all visions are due to chance; there is always an element of faith to science. *Phantasms of the Living* proposed that ghosts are hallucinatory events because of their "complete or almost complete failure to leave any physical traces behind them, and [because of] the fact that they occasionally behave in ways impossible to physical objects." The analysis of these cases, as well as the scientific, almost obsessive approach Gurney adopted in his research, is impressive—step by step, he follows any and every thread of logic that might illuminate the data, identifying several possible ways that the "machinery" of hallucinations "may be set in motion."

*One day, after having spent a considerable time in inspecting a village churchyard, what was my horror and consternation to find, on leaving it, that wherever my eyes rested I could descry nothing but monumental inscriptions. The dust on the roadside somehow seemed to form itself into letters. The macadamized highway seemed written all over with mourning, lamentation, and woe: and even when I turned my gaze to the stone dykes on either side of the way, it was only to find that, by some subtle chemistry of my brain, the weather-stains and cracks shaped themselves into words which I could plainly decipher, and found to be of the same nature as those which I had recently been reading in the churchyard. Every time*

*that autumn and winter that I paid a visit to a churchyard, the experience recurred; and on more than one occasion also without that exciting cause.*
*Rev. Robertson Wilson*


Death, flight, illness, signs—we do not always see what we wish to. When discussing optical hallucinations, Gurney writes, "With the sane, a large number consist in the casual vision—an *after-image*, as we might say—of a near relative or familiar associate," indicating a hallucination's probable (though not necessarily intentional) relationship with memory or recognition. "Hallucinations of the senses . . . may be defined as *percepts which lack, but which can only by distinct reflection be recognized as lacking, the objective basis which they suggest.*" A false circuit. "Sometimes hallucinations begin . . . with a glow of light. Sometimes they are just *there*, and are only known to be hallucinations because they unaccountably vanish. Those who perceive them may feel . . . sensations of intense cold, 'electrical thrills,' prickling in the scalp, or faintness."


The most common cases of visual hallucinations, continued Gurney, are of a single object. Like the experience of reoccurring nightmares, so too do hallucinations often focus on a particular image or scene. A phantom cat on the staircase, tombstone inscriptions, or a lone stranger waiting for you in the road. "We might compare this locality to a kaleidoscope, which when shaken is capable of turning out a certain limited number of combinations." *No man. Just space. Honking cars behind me.*

Your eyes sliced open, the top film pulled off—it forms two rings and a perfect circle of blindness. You are reminded. One morning, caught in a crowd on the El to work, you saw a person across the way melt out of sight. Just one human shape in the vapor; the outline of a man decaying. First dumbness struck, then utter blankness left a slowly shutting vision. Shoving toward open train doors you stumbled out, felt faint.

"When we hallucinate, we take ourselves to be perceiving, *and perceptions themselves have a felt reality.*" As you searched for a place to sit, sight gradually abandoned you. Then panic arrived as a circle of absolute darkness encroaching upon a crescent of florescent light. "The eye is the first circle; the horizon which it forms is the second; and throughout nature this primary figure is repeated without end." Bright train beams shimmered and shook. Stars sparkled in the mirror of your stare. You watched as the taillights blasted from the back of the El, disappearing quickly into the tunnel, hazy pixels in fade.

After years of obsessively collecting, Gurney was all too aware of the monotony of the information going into *Phantasms of the Living.* Individually the stories might have held little scientific worth but as a collection Gurney knew he was onto something. En masse the evidence was astounding. Time after time the accounts demonstrated that people around the world were experiencing similar visions of apparitions, ghosts, and disembodied voices. Gurney, a naturally skeptical man, found himself putting faith in such odd resemblances. "The emerging pattern [was] derived from number and repetition, in the way that so many stories of the dead [echo] each other . . . by their weird consistency." Like William James, Gurney had spent his early years as an artist and was only much later attracted to scientific research out of a curiosity—about the unknown, the invisible—that could not be satisfied solely through artistic process.

A restless man, prone to periods of intense depression, Gurney went to school for medicine and law, eventually tiring of both fields. From there he turned to the philosophy of music and published a book on musical theory and aesthetics entitled *The Power of Sound*. Gurney's "readiness to explore the musically unusual was paralleled by a general love of speculation and enquiry, and a complete disrespect for conventional lines of thought." Later, when he met Myers, Gurney was drawn to the idea of collecting tangible "proof" of ethereal, inexplicable feelings or ideas. The purpose of *Phantasms of the Living* became to gather as many statements as possible. To describe "the supernatural events that [the SPR] deemed credible [about five percent of all reports gathered] . . . and to put them in perspective, reinforcing their 'evidence' with theories that might explain it and arguments to support those theories." Myers and Gurney, along with their recruit, Frank Podmore, "wanted the book to be so good, so compelling . . . that it would sway the world."

At night, too, circles rule. The moon: a slowly shutting eye too drained to open. Each stoplight rushes toward you—speeding halos—sure warning that nothing exists in the periphery to help guide the vehicle you maneuver. Possible side effects include: "glare, seeing halos around images, difficulty driving at night, fluctuating vision." The crooked, poorly marked lane. Unknowable sinkholes. Other vehicles rush by—aiming flashing orbs at your eyes—two from across the lane, two more in each of three mirrors.

Do you dare close your eyes and attempt to drive by memory? Rely on the patterns of the street, or on the laws of space imagined? No. A vision implies the future. What you see in front of you is what you're headed both toward and away from. A vision is sight, of course, but also a measure of knowledge. "Are you pretty well—have you been happy— / Are your Eyes safe?"

If only you could predict for sure what lies ahead: the next lap of the track. If only you could intuit what is about to rush right through you or what has undoubtedly already been here. The fear of driving at night is a constant refusal. You will not steer into rubble or become a permanent passenger, a child strapped in, suffering care. You do not wish to go nowhere—becoming a not-force, not-presence, a voice that does not protest the image when there is none—asking, *What is the terror that holds me home?* After all, the road has ghosts of its own and the occasion comes upon you to question the worth of an aggressive imagination. *The man did not exist—my lying eyes invited him.*

The evidence in *Phantasms of the Living* relies upon the honesty of those who were interviewed, a fact that was considered when reviewing the material. The book is filled with disclaimers, assumptions of miscalculation, and acknowledgments of the possibility of human error in memory or motive. It includes descriptions of Gurney's own biases, personal assumptions, tendencies. His goal in amassing the cases was not to discover an absolute truth but to present evidence, confirm paranormal events with objective reports, and produce an encyclopedic collection of eyewitness accounts. A process of accumulation.

Many of the accounts in *Phantasms* (as well as in the later *Proceedings of the Society for Psychical Research*) are superficially uneventful. Fabrications, exaggerations, hyperbole, lies; deceit, insanity, dreaming. Gurney would weed some out, let others stand. There is always an element of faith to science. "But the definition of spiritual should be that which has its own evidence." A scientist must at once maintain an interest in research and a "distrust [of] the facts and inferences."

Despite some troubles the resulting study is thrilling, both in what it indicates about sane hallucinations and what it reveals about the power of testimony as evidence. In *The Founders of Psychical Research*, Alan Gauld writes, "Since Gurney's time every serious discussion of crisis apparitions has taken its start from his classification and arrangement of them. To pass from even the ablest of previous works to *Phantasms of the Living* is like passing from a mediaeval bestiary or herbal to Linnaeus's *Systema Naturae*." In *Lectures on Psychical Research*, C. D. Broad warns against the common misconception of a hallucination as something that implies "that the person who has it is at the time in a *pathological condition*." Both Gurney and the SPR were especially interested in veridical hallucinations, or those that occur in sound minds and yet demonstrate "future events or apparently unknowable present realities."

Premonition, divination, forecast—an experience in which "there did exist, at about the time when such an hallucinatory quasi-perception occurred, at a certain one place in the world a certain person in a certain state and in certain surroundings, so peculiar and so closely correlated in detail with the content of the experience that it is difficult or impossible to believe that the coexistent in time and the correlation in detail can be purely contingent." Not all visions are due to chance.

In your car, you accelerate into the shadow of the image. You glide farther down the dark road. "[S]ee the shadowy lines of its trees, / And catch, in sudden gleams, / The sheen of the far-surrounding seas . . ." Apparitions, or sane hallucinations, "occur . . . most often in states of relaxation, sometimes in fatigue, sometimes in anxiety but very seldom in active grief; and usually to people who were alone at the time." *The whole thing was so vivid, and the street was particularly quiet at the time.* In the coffin of your car you are protected.

Cones can separate lanes—others divide the eye. "For it is only natural that images should assume the unwonted vividness of sensations especially at those moments when the external organs of sense are not occupied with *other* sensations." Suppose the phantoms in the road are not anxiety but the prediction of a crisis actually happening? Here, at another time, a crash occurred, or elsewhere, right now, a violence. You can only look over and over. Bright beams shimmer and shake—stars sparkle in the mirror of your stare.

The doctor's office has set up a system by which family members can witness your surgical procedure from the short distance of the waiting room: tape, laser, slice, shape, reattach, finish. Arms tied down, neck covered, your torso lies flat on the operating table, head unable to move in a headrest that is angled toward the floor, immobile. Your body waits, frozen. Your mother is there—she'll drive you home—and now her eyes, outside the room, are focused on the monitor's screen. She sees the lids of your corneas cut, recurved, replaced upon new rings. Her eyes focus on yours—the image is conveyed through space by one lens intent upon the center of another. She monitors the science of your blindness.

Of course, you see nothing. She's not here, not anywhere immediately near, but somehow you feel her presence because you sense her looking. The closest physical comparison to a hallucination is probably dreaming. Both phenomena include the sensations of reality without the so-called truth. "We know that the sort of day-dream which comes nearest to hallucinations is favored by *repose* of the sense-organs; that when we want to call up the vivid image of a scene, to make it as real—as sensorial—as possible, we close our eyes." Or as yours are: open but stripped of gaze. Spot a human shape in the road—you're already hurtling forward.

A vision is sight, but also a measure of knowledge. While in surgery, you imagine bright deer eyes speckling the side of the street, two leaping across the shoulder. Once, when younger, you crashed a car and the windshield shattered all over. A disastrous wreck, the car totaled, and forever after nightmares of killing your brothers. Imagined scenes always occur like this: slow-motion mental pictures. "Dreams are by far the most familiar instances of the projection by the mind of images that are mistaken for realities: indeed, it is just because they are so familiar, and waking hallucinations comparatively so rare, that there is a danger of overlooking the psychological identity of the two classes. We might call dreams the normal form of hallucination, or waking hallucinations the pathological form of dreaming..."

Shortly after the publication of *Phantasms of the Living*, which was met with little critical review, Edmund Gurney died while on a mission to investigate a haunted house in Brighton. It was 1888. There were rumors of suicide. Inspired by Gurney's beginnings and devastated by the incomplete work he left behind, the Society for Psychical Research sanctioned an official investigation entitled "Census of Hallucinations." "The universe is fluid and volatile. Permanence is but a word of degrees." The census asked members of the SPR to gather local and regional evidence of "casual hallucinations of sane persons, including . . . phantasmal appearances which some deny to be hallucinations because they believe them to be ghosts."

William James explained the census in a letter addressed to SPR members asking for their research and input. He wrote,

"The object of our enquiry is (1) to ascertain approximately the *proportion of persons* who have such experiences, and (2) to obtain details as to the experiences with a view to examining into their cause and meaning." The goal was to approach mystery with an objective eye. To amass a democratic and straightforward set of stories. "The most that could be done with every reported case has been done," wrote James. "The witnesses, where possible, have been cross-examined personally, the collateral facts have been looked up, and the narrative appears with its precise coefficient of evidential worth stamped on it, so that all may know just what its weight as proof may be. Outside of these Proceedings, I know of no systematic attempt to *weigh* the evidence for the supernatural."

The process of collecting information lasted from 1889 to 1897 and resulted in a wealth of firsthand accounts from England, France, Germany, Russia, Brazil, and the United States. The study's evidence suggested that over ten percent of the people polled had experienced some manner of waking, or "sane," hallucination. Many of these were considered crisis apparitions, or "phantasms of the dead," and included sightings of people who had just died or were about to. "The British census was the largest—17,000 surveyed—and the American study . . . was second, with 7,123. All concluded that death-day apparitions occurred in startling numbers. The American survey found that these 'ghosts' occurred at 487 times the rate predicted by chance." William James insisted that "if the Society could continue to exist long enough for the public to become familiar with its presence, so that any case of apparition or of a house or person infested with unaccountable noises or disturbances of material objects would, as a matter of course, be reported to its officers, who thereupon would take down the evidence in as thorough a way as possible, we should end ere long by having a mass of facts concrete enough to found a decent theory upon."

*December, 1884.*

*On the afternoon of Sunday, December 18th, 1864, my father-in-law, Mr. B., my husband, and I were sitting in the dining-room at D. Hall. The room was a large one . . . on one side was the fireplace, with a door at each side; opposite the fireplace were three windows; standing with your back to the fireplace, at the end of the room on your right were two more windows, and on your left a blank wall. These windows were some height from the ground, probably 7 ft. or more, so that no one could look in unless standing on a chair. It was dark, and we were sitting round the fire, the shutters not having been closed. . . . Suddenly Mr. B. said, 'Who is that looking in at the window?' pointing to the furthest of the two windows. We laughed, knowing that no one could look in, as there was nothing there for them to stand on. Mr. B. persisted in his assertion, saying that it was a woman with a pale face and black hair; that the face was familiar to him, but he could not remember her name; and he insisted on my husband going round the outside of the house one way, whilst he went the other. They, however, saw no one . . . . The time was 5:45 p.m.*

*On the following Tuesday I heard of the death of my mother . . . who had died at St. Peter's Port . . .* exactly at 5:45 p.m. on December 18th, *the hour at which the face appeared at the window.*

*E. A. B.*

To see is to expect the past. It is to permit or capture what once stood in front of you. A vision is sight, of course, but also a measure of knowledge. "Invisible, indivisible Spirit, / how is it you come so near . . ."

During the procedure you imagine the look of eyes as they're open—"small glassy disks with an agate-like rim . . . like sea-pebbles in the grip of a starfish." Ripples, rings, hoops, haloes. "Something seen in the imagination or . . . supernatural." A vision is circular in shape—with no end, only spin—the expansion or narrowing of focus. "The natural world may be conceived of as a system of concentric circles, and we now and then detect in nature slight dislocations, which apprize us that this surface on which we now stand is not fixed, but sliding." Where have you heard these words before? Are the images you witness merely yet to occur?

Intended to correct missed steps, blurred beams, oft-mistaken lines. Intended to result in the clarity that is present for others. To prevent running into walls, falling down, misjudging where the lane is as you're driving into town. Reshaped eyes—the tissue ablated—will result in clearer eyesight, less haze, firmer signage. No more off-objects, misplaced faces, erroneous contexts. It is a minor procedure.

Rising from darkness into an unfamiliar landscape you are afraid to move in the absence of reference. Your body behaves in strange ways. When sight returns, it crashes back. Two bright white surgical lights shoot straight into your skull. The world is held at a distance. Slowly, as you attempt to rise from the table, your limbs go numb, as though caught in the center of a street staring down a driver. There's no car, just space, two lights aiming straight at you.

# A Pickle for the Knowing Ones

On a Saturday morning in early November of 1993 the Libertyville Wildcats, a crew of orange-and-black-clad teenagers,
amassed themselves—sweaty, excited, perched awkwardly on
slick-backed plastic chairs—in the high school cafeteria for a
pregame pep talk by Dale Christensen, their beloved leader
and the school's football coach of twenty-one years. The Wildcats were about to board a bus to the nearby Chicago suburb of
Wilmette in order to compete against Loyola Academy in the
state semifinal playoff game and it is reasonable to imagine the
ensuing speech as the sort of saccharine sermon-like monologue seen in late-eighties sports movies or perhaps even a
tear-jerking diatribe such as those delivered by Coach Eric
Taylor on *Friday Night Lights*. It was a bright day—damp and
muddy—not quite the severe bite of a typical Illinois winter.
As is customary in these occasions, Christensen would have

lauded his young players' mammoth talent, their cunning athletic prowess, and their absolute and undoubted ability to *crush* the opposing team. He would have spoken of future glory, finely honed instincts, and the fame that would soon befall their beautiful boyish heads. Perhaps they even bowed these boyish heads, sans helmets, to pray in a moment of divine recognition.

What is certain, according to *The New York Times* and *Chicago Tribune* as well as half a dozen local newspapers, is that sometime during the middle of this speech the heavy doors of the cafeteria swung open and an unidentified boy, another teenager, ran into the room and past the crowd of bulky young men to shoot Dale Christensen at point-blank range in the chest. What followed was chaos. Some of the students hid in bathroom stalls while others rushed to call the police or fled the building in panic. Reed Christensen, the coach's son as well as a 225-pound junior-year star linebacker, was quoted as shouting "My dad's been shot!" as the other coaches hurried to clear the room of students and emergency vehicles sped to the scene of the crime. This was the autumn before my family moved to Libertyville, nine months before I would matriculate, and six years before the Columbine High School massacre, a brink-of-the-century American tragedy that would usher in a previously unforeseen and interminable nightmare of school shootings after which no parent or pupil could ever again think of school as a safe space. In 1993, however, there were no security guards at LHS—no known need for ALICE training yet—just a room of terrified kids and orange painted paw prints indicating the stamped path of a cartoon wildcat. What was revealed to the public only after the building had cleared, after the team had reluctantly, dejectedly boarded the bus and played the game (with a final score of 27–14 including 23 total penalties and Reed Christensen getting ejected from the game for un-sportsmanlike conduct), was that Coach Christensen had staged his own shooting. He had *faked his own death* (the blood was ketchup, the gun a starter pistol that fired blanks) in an attempt to motivate the Wildcats to win a high school football game and proceed to State in his honor. Years later when I found myself relaying this insane tale to a group of friends at a party it occurred to me—in one of those flashes of self-aware-ness that only arise while standing in a room of half-buzzed acquaintances waiting patiently for another drink or the con-clusion of the narrative—that there was no way this story could be true, that I must have misunderstood the details described to me years earlier by my younger brothers and consequently embellished the plot in ways that would serve my own sensibil-ity. The following morning, I decided to investigate the case and discovered a wealth of even more disturbing specifics in the original reporting. News sources declared that which I had already known through secondhand accounts and I was stunned not only by the accuracy of the seemingly made-up facts as I had repeated them but also by the new and previous-ly unknown sea of wild particulars that roiled to the surface as I pursued these professional and verifiable versions. According to several sources, Christensen was infamous for this type of antic; he once asked players to attack a fuel-soaked dummy (clothed as a member of the opposing team) after he couldn't make it light on fire; his nickname was, incredibly, "Crazy"; and the *Chicago Tribune* Sports section quoted Christensen as claiming that "at Libertyville, we put a premium on psycho-physiological stamina." In another *Tribune* piece Christensen confessed to having practiced a similar prank on his wife as an April Fool's joke but that "knowing [his] reputation for crazy stunts" she was unaffected by the performance. "That's why I tried for more realism this time," he said, "except, this was an errant lesson plan that went awry." There were other more harrowing layers of detail, such as the fact that Christensen had chosen one of the very few African American students at the high school to play the role of the "shooter" (claiming that the original actor—a theater student—had gone out of town and was unavailable), or the troubling statement from senior lineman Mike Duffy in which he said, "obviously, the shock of the idea we were going to die overshadowed any point [Christensen] was trying to make." I was astonished to find that even the seemingly fictional and clichéd detail concerning the blood—*ketchup packets*—was verifiable among the winding tracks of archived digital print, as was the quote from Christensen's son, causing a brick of guilt to settle in my stomach when I realized I had exploited a kid's alarm for the sake of entertainment. Of course, I also knew the facts as they were documented were most likely skewed, played down, or managed by the other coaches and a handful of students who adored him. *Why not?* one might ask, in context. There is an element of awful prankster charm to the hoax and who else but a high school football coach (that living symbol of leadership, that hero to the American masses) could have gotten away with it? By the time I arrived in Libertyville as a freshman the following September, Christensen had been stripped of his coaching duties but still somehow retained employment as our driver's ed instructor and I have vague memories of him pacing the perimeter of the orange-and-cream fluorescent-lit gym. When I went looking for other examples of people faking (or attempting to fake) their own death—(wondering if our options really are *to be* or *not to be* or *to pretend not to be*)—I was impressed by two other stories that were similarly based in— what was obviously from the outside—outrageous male ego, learning that other than running from the law this seemed the most common provocation. The first of these stories—which was published in *Gawker* in September of 2012 and also appeared as a bit in NPR's "Wait, Wait Don't Tell Me"—was the brief account of a thirty-year-old Russian man who orchestrated the scene of his own violent and explosive end via car crash, replete with a "mangled car . . . ambulances, smoke, and carnage." When his girlfriend, who had been summoned to the production, arrived frantic and panicked, she was told that her lover had died in the wreck, shortly after which he rose on cue from the blood and ashes of his dramatized demise to propose marriage. The article quotes the man, a youthful Alexey Bykov, as (one can only imagine *proudly*) explaining: "I wanted her to realize how empty her life would be without me and how life would have no meaning without me." The second story that caught my eye occurred in the early 1800s when Lord Timothy Dexter of Newburyport, Massachusetts (the "Lord" title was both self-proclaimed and baseless) pretended to die so that he might design his own funeral (for which the entire village was invited via an ad in the newspaper) as well as gauge the level of grief his wife would perform at his passing. One might gain a sense of "Lord" Dexter's vanity by reading a bit of his memoir, *A Pickle for the Knowing Ones: Or, Plain Truths in a Homespun Dress* (1802), in which he rejects punctuation and traditional spelling (later proposing that a reader may "salt" the text with commas where they please) and un-self-consciously blathers on about his occasionally enchanting if totally delusional personal philosophies regarding politics, healthy living, citizenship, and democracy. Apparently, when Dexter observed his wife only mildly sniffling at his coffin-side (the funeral ceremony was performed in the home garden where Dexter had previously commissioned statues of legendary men including George Washington, Thomas Jefferson, Napoleon Bonaparte, and . . . himself), from where he watched (in an upstairs attic?), he judged her sorrow to be less rich than anticipated—her psyche not sufficiently *undone*—and promptly stomped downstairs, exposing the ruse, to beat her. Is it always love that spawns such ludicrous cruelty? Or is the incentive in this case to witness another's life obliterated by the end of your own? Dale Christensen's logic, one imagines, was that the Libertyville Wildcats would play harder for the win, that that they would fight *in his honor*, and that he would go down in history as their fearless leader or so-called Captain. What no one including myself knew at the time of the fake shooting was that my own father would die, almost to the day, a decade later in the same suburb just a few miles away. I would hold his hand and see his last breath. Sometimes I wonder if Dale's son, who from what I recall was not "in" on the "trick," still startles awake in the middle of the night drenched in the kind of dread-sweat one forever suffers after such an awful shock. His father's joke was both grotesque and amusing—impossible, outrageous, immoral—the perfect party tale—and it never fails to remind me

that when I was in high school I didn't try at all to disguise the disdain I harbored for our, I thought, ironically named town and for my teenage peers who (so I felt in my most predictably melancholic moments) were myopically focused on sports scores and generic crushes. I didn't reject these activities exactly but *at least*—I would tell myself repeatedly—*I wouldn't stay here forever.* Nothing that happened to me in that place, at that age, felt right—little seemed real—but for some inexplicable and quite likely psychologically revealing reason when I recall Libertyville, the location that I cite as "home," I never disclose an anecdote from experience but instead the story of Christensen—told to me by my brothers years later, after all three of us had graduated—which seems to provide evidence of some ominous thing I had sensed all along. Many years later I came across an essay by the art critic and feminist scholar Lucy Lippard who wrote that the search for a home is "the mythical search for the *axis mundi*, for a center, for some place to stand, for something to hang on to," and remember reading about Lippard's rejection of home as an idealized permanent place or a given, inherited thing, her explanation being that one's exploration of their past is circular, archeological, flawed, and collaborative—that there are no linear narratives in memory and therefore the supposed twenty-first-century home is not a singular location of safety and salvation (a constant point to forever flee from; to return to; the source of inspiration and response; of rage and nostalgia) but instead a transformative, multifaceted, and fractional idea. A spiral or loop. An arrangement of stories. Home, to Lippard, is an idea that can only be understood through persistent and specific—local—investiga-

tion and an interrogation of the fluctuating communities that surround one. Perhaps most interesting of all are Lippard's studies of alternative mobile home structures (or "wheel estate") and how they simultaneously express the oh-so-American ideals of ownership, luxury, and perpetual motion. She suggests that related to these roving residencies—at least for artists and writers—is the tendency to reject or destroy a dwelling, which recalls me to both Gordon Matta-Clark's 1974 piece *Splitting* (in which he carefully slices an abandoned house in half, allowing a thin sliver of natural light to puncture the dim interior space as if a flash of dawn through the door jamb) and also the infamous Iowa City farmhouse where I once knew generations of writers to have lived in chaos and squalor. The farmhouse, once situated on Muscatine Street, south of town and past the VFW, was a legendary residence in which writers—so the rumors go—wrote, fought, fucked, partied, and in general never recovered. I recall Z., who in 2006 was among the last batch of writers to reside there, showing me the eviction notice from the landlord which was replete with a list of the various damages that had accrued over the course of more than a decade: piles of trash and dirty mattresses, sludge in the sinks, holes in the walls, a moldy dishwasher, busted limbs of ancient furniture, old clothes, boxes of manuscripts, rotting food, neglected paperbacks, broken instruments, dead plants, deflated bike tires, soggy towels, mildew, grime, blood, dirt, dust, rust, and semen—with the total cost taken out of the deposit something like a hundred dollars. Apparently, the family who owned the house simply showed up one day and repossessed it, cut the wings into sections, tied them to truck beds, and bore the structure away (some say it traveled just down the street and others claim it was carried to North Carolina). Lippard warns that to make too much of the past "fosters a determinism that limits the future." When I eventually left Libertyville for college I assumed I'd seldom return and when, senior year, my father was diagnosed with an aggressive terminal cancer it was a shock to spend so much time in the place where I'd once attended high school. During the months in which his health declined I haunted our house—looming in the doorways of empty rooms, looping hallways, pacing up and down the driveway or steering along suburban roads in a thoughtless fog to the pharmacy—while he underwent chemo and my family attempted to refuse the one basic truth that was hurtling toward us. Shortly after his death—which occurred nine months later on a bright November morning—I made an impulsive decision to move to Prague with S., a friend from high school, who had grown up just down the street from me and was traveling to the Czech Republic to teach English. I attempted to escape the realities of grief by following S. across the ocean and can honestly now recall very little of the logic of it. While I was absent—drinking absinthe and smoking hash, living near the National Gallery in Holesovice, on the third floor of a loft whose wide screenless windows swung open above the market—my younger brother P., whom I had been living with in Chicago, sublet my room to an old acquaintance of his from a suburb near the one we grew up in. D., the subletter, was someone he had known, not well, for years, and the kind of amiable guy—a little older than P.—who would presumably pay his portion of the rent on time. I had fled Chicago without a second thought for who would occupy my space those months I traveled. What possessed and terrorized my waking mind was the sudden loss of my father, which manifested itself not so much as a fact but an unyielding numbness that I would only fully comprehend when, years later, like a mountain of mud shoveled off of my chest, the pressure lifted and I could feel again the familiar fit of my life around me. Perhaps it is for this reason that I cannot say for sure when P.

first began having trouble with his new roommate; it's possible that I didn't know the details until later. In any case, when he tells the story now, P. begins with the moment, a few months in, when D. asked to borrow his car. P. handed him his keys and when a day went by without seeing D. again he assumed his roommate had driven to the suburbs to visit his mother. Two days passed and then a week, so said P., but he wasn't especially worried because D. was supposedly, everyone thought (irrationally, superficially), *reliable*—he was from the same place we were, he was harmless and perhaps a bit arrogant—with his J. Crew sweaters, his boat shoes and khaki pants—he was clean-shaven and witty and, sure, occasionally a bit sketchy, perhaps an addict, condescending to women, but those *bright eyes* and *button-up shirts*—he seemed dependable. And thus there was a brief attempt on the part of P. to track down D. who had seemingly vanished into thin air. The threat of danger slowly dissolved into annoyance—was D. hiding?, was he lying?, could he really have stolen P.'s car?—when my brother, so far from where I was, received a letter in the mail requesting his presence at the county jail in order to collect his used burgundy Pontiac from storage. It turned out D. borrowed the car to drive to court where he was then found guilty of whatever crimes he committed, sending P.'s car to the holding lot. The story resumes months later upon my return when I discovered someone else's possessions crowding my bedroom, since D. never returned to collect his things. P. helped me clean out the room and I remember that we were shocked (and inspired? horrified—but delighted?) by the idea of someone—*someone we knew*—leaving all of their property behind; shocked by the possibility that a person could *choose* to disappear so completely, hurling forward into a fresh life that did not, in this case, include D.'s computer, his expensive sweaters and jackets (some of which my brother, a poor college student at the time, pulled out of the Goodwill bags and kept for himself), his toothbrush, his novels, several pairs of leather shoes, his... *home brewing kit?*, ski boots, random notes and phone numbers, a basketball, a box of condoms, and finally a handful of bullets which I discovered between the mattress and box spring of the bed next to a gun-sized negative space in the cushion. I remember wondering what essential connection ever prevents one from abandoning their life: *why stay?* the essential question. Years later, I discovered Doug Richmond's 1986 book, *How To Disappear Completely and Never Be Found*, an amateur treatise on purposefully disappearing, in which Richmond details the reasons a man might flee his responsibilities, including sensible tips on how to accomplish this feat. In a section entitled "Boredom & Frustration," Richmond writes, "there is something about the middle years of life, the forties to fifties, that makes a man take a long, hard look at himself, his works, and his future." This "hard look" often results, so writes Richmond, in a desire to vacate, start anew, or "commit the 'revocable suicide' and disappear with the thought that [one] will leave their troubles behind." Richmond's casual tone (in contrast to the fairly sophisticated, deeply gendered, and possibly criminal nature of the task at hand) captivated my attention with idiotic statements like: "I've come to the conclusion that perhaps it is the men who *don't* disappear who should be pitied," and I abandoned the book before finishing in a restless quest for more specific information than what Richmond could provide. My brother P.'s bizarre narrative picks up again when, several years later, he was trudging through a colossal Chicago snow-storm, pushing his way toward an El stop and struggling to cross a small traffic-free street through a wall of heavy flakes when a car came skidding around the corner and the driver slammed on the brakes mere moments before hitting him. The air was sharp, the snow severe, and a solitary streetlamp cast a single circle of orange light to the side of the scene like a poorly aimed spotlight. The next moment is challenging to describe—it scarcely sounds real—but P. insists that when D., who was, incredibly, the driver, hurled open the car door to angrily assault whomever had obstructed his course he saw my brother standing there dressed *in his old clothes* as if a physical manifestation of his discarded past. D.'s life was doubled, creased in an instant, and the two young men froze facing each other in the blizzard's mirror. D.—whose expression, as I imagine it, rapidly shifted from anger to panic—took a few steps back, sank into the car (one can't help but wonder *whose* car?), and sped away, *really*, so said P., never to be seen again. Every time this story is told I'm reminded of how possible it is to transform one's identity merely by shifting locations—our selves recognizable mostly in context—so that "home" perhaps most honestly refers to the space created by those who have observed the most various versions of your character the longest. Such were my thoughts when one rainy autumn afternoon I barreled south on 294 from Milwaukee to Chicago, heading back into the city after a family event in Wisconsin. The trip took me in the direction of the exit that, if I were to get off the highway, would lead into Libertyville and past the cemetery where my father was buried. I was exhausted and hungry, my nerves shot, and the windshield thrummed with the dull percussion of water on glass. I considered how—in a previous, now less familiar time and place—my father had explained to me on a similar trip the appeal of Janis Joplin's scratchy voice and the eccentric pleasure of Meatloaf; I recalled his five-day beard, his preoccupied gaze, and how he would sneeze every time he ate wintergreen. I remembered the story of my dad launching water balloons from the roof of a Madison dorm room and him mixing cement for a terrace. I recalled his steady hands, winter skiing, and how, as a little girl, I perched behind his drawing board at work, pretending to be an engineer like he was. I thought of how I'd heard—never from him—how he was the only person to witness the death of his older sister. I remembered the worst of his sweaters, his high school pictures, and how one time, my mother tells me, when I was young and couldn't walk yet, I hurled my feeble baby body

down a flight of stairs because I could, so she claims, hear his voice from the bottom. Because I could, so she says, not bear to be apart. But now . . . *now* . . . how would he know me? I banished the thought. I drove right by the exit and I didn't stop. I'd give anything to see my father again but that doesn't mean I can ever go back there.

# Alphabet

I suppose it's true, I'll tell you, that years ago I encountered a
young man at a dive bar in Copenhagen who—after sipping
his pilsner and tilting in close—explained, unprompted (in the
manner of young men explaining, unprompted, in dive bars
the whole world over) that there was actually a *much better* dive
bar than the one my companions and I were lurking in, a bar
that would remain open all night, a bar not far from here, so
he said, and since we were new to the city, since it was in fact
our first night in the city, he and his friends would be pleased
to escort us, if we were so inclined, to this second location,
this *other better dive bar*, at which point, as if an afterthought,
he divulged the kind of pleasing and preposterous non sequitur that seems only ever to grace a stranger when he followed
his offer to lead us to liquor by claiming to have once been a
famous Danish soprano and the singer responsible for hitting

the high notes in Lars von Trier's musical *Dancer in the Dark*, starring Björk. It sounded implausible but not impossible. We followed him to the second location. The lot of us—my brother and a few friends—had just arrived from Amsterdam where we had consumed large amounts of shawarma, marveled at Hendrick Avercamp's low-lit *Winter Landscape with Ice Skaters*, and celebrated the dawn of 2012 from a garage-sized open window in the red-light district, which was that night replete with shrieking teens and frantic tourists, and where a relentless series of fireworks detonated at such alarming rates that the ensuing flames and smoldering vehicles might have deceived any random drifter into thinking they had entered a war zone. Although the trip's impetus was distinct from my research I was pleased when it included a week in Copenhagen, the home and final resting place of recently deceased Danish poet Inger Christensen, author of *alphabet*, a book-length naturalist epic, which begins: "apricot trees exist, apricot trees exist," and subsequently lists in a visionary repetitive reverie all manner of flora, fauna, and phenomena: "bracken exists; and blackberries, blackberries; / bromine exists; and hydrogen, hydrogen;" "guns and wailing women, full as / greedy owls exist; the scene of the crime exists; / the scene of the crime." Translated into English in 2000 by Susanna Nied (the book was originally published in 1981), *alphabet* is bound by two major limits ("given limits exist"): the alphabet and the Fibonacci sequence, which is the mathematical expression of a spiral and a frequent pattern in the natural world: snail shells, fern leaves, pineapple scales, pinecones, hurricanes, seed heads, animal flight, galaxies, and even, I recently read, the human face and a healthy uterus. The equation, related to the golden ratio, begins as most things do, in nothing (zed, zero, zilch), becoming—with a conceptual leap that feels unbearable—*something*, or *one*, at which point each new numeral is the sum of the two that proceed it: 0, 1, 1, 2, 3, 5, 8, 13, 21, etc. Christensen uses the form in conjunction with the alphabet so that the first section of the book (beginning with "a" for apricot) is one line while the second ("b" for bracken, blackberries, bromine) is a couplet, and so on until the sections stop at "n" (the letter representing whole numbers and the beginning of *nuclear, nature,* or *nothing*). The book harnesses a form that never escapes itself or fully concludes and grows to serve as a metaphor for memory's erasure by accretion. The poem is an ever-amassing acknowledgement of the elements of the world—our world, Christensen's world—that *exist* (her foremost refrain) and as the images build slowly, systematically—like the measured introduction of instruments in Ravel's *Bolero*—they also turn away from the predominantly organic

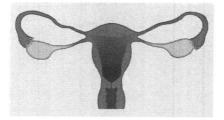

("cicadas exist; chicory, chromium") toward the violent ("atom bombs exist // Hiroshima, Nagasaki // Hiroshima, August / 6th, 1945") back to the human ("love exists, love exists / your hand a baby bird so obliviously tucked / into mine") and the visionary ("snow / is not snow at all / when it snows / in mid-June") always managing—as would any natural spiral achieving revolution—to involve the strands of its own generation ("don't panic; it's bracken on a / trip, gathering time and / binding it; bracken"). Christensen's poem can be read as a furious pre-apocalyptic documentary response to the nuclear fear and Cold War dread of her time (a dread that has since escalated) in which the word "exist" becomes its own ghostly opposite— material that *doesn't* or *hasn't* or *won't ever again* endure (polar bears?, kingfishers?, shrubs?, children!?!?)—illuminating the poem's violence as well as—*by the very act of writing*—erasing each recorded idea or object and what it signifies. In one section Christensen leads the reader on an expedition around the world by connecting each body of water or land mass to its neighbor ("around the Barents Sea / the water stops at / Spitzbergen / and just behind / Spitzbergen / ice drifts in the / Arctic Ocean / and just behind the / Arctic Ocean / there's solid ice at the / North Pole . . .") until she has imagined her way, in a few traceable steps, around the globe name-by-name, demonstrating how irrevocably connected one nation (one population, one landscape, one citizen) is to another. Much of *alphabet* is concerned with the space between experience and extinction—the cataloguing of what currently *is* or can be perceived and therefore *eradicated*—and we begin to understand her nouns as apparitions of their reference, recalling Jacques Derrida's claim in *The Animal That Therefore I Am* that "every case of naming involves announcing a death to come in the surviving of a ghost." Christensen's poem is a dirge and hymn, a chronicling of potential in its breaking. Even the initial image, that infamous apricot tree—which I realized the week I spent in Copenhagen wouldn't have thrived in Christensen's city—contains a hazardous seed in the form of a pit that is poisonous if eaten in quantity, causing symptoms similar to cyanide poisoning. I have always read this line as Christensen's proof that nature's systems shield signs and, possibly, a nod to the fact that in order to accelerate our own extinction we might one day pray for an apricot tree (or two, or three) to have survived and for their seeds, upon digestion, to liberate us from what will certainly be an unmanageably bleak apocalypse. One might compare Christensen's use of natural forms to that of Howardena Pindell's *Untitled, 1969–1970*, a mixed-media 4×3 square-net sculpture made of rolled canvas, or Robert Rohm's deceptively simple *Rope Piece*, which was originally formed in 1969 of heavy shipping lines and knots nailed to the gallery wall in a strict grid and then, according to the Des Moines Arts Center's wall plaque, "cut or unfastened at predetermined points [Rohm] had plotted in a preliminary diagram" illuminating the "tension" between "rationality and randomness." I saw the piece one morning in Iowa years after the trip to

Copenhagen during a brief stop along an extended drive out west and it reminded me of the "invisible architecture" (as Barbara Guest would call it) of *alphabet*. Like Christensen, who said that "by using a system you are trying to reveal the rhythm of the universe," Rohm is known to have employed

mathematical and geometric structures to attract disarray and acknowledge the man-made disruption of scientific systems. Although one can't help but admire Rohm's damaged and beautiful parallel lines and their echo of fishing nets, spiderwebs, and desert fences, there is something quite literally hypnotizing in the spin of the spiral, perhaps even more so, in my opinion, than in the most hallowed and elegant of all shapes, the *circle*, which Emerson claims is "the first of all forms" and which the spiral imitates in concept while also involving infinitely new territory as it expands, serving as a spring into the past and future, or possibly even a third dimension. These forms were on my mind the summer of 2015 when O. and I visited Robert Smithson's forty-five-year-old earthworks project, Spiral Jetty, on our way west to Nevada and ultimately the Pacific Coast. In order to visit the piece one must first find their way to a particular point on the northeast shore of the Great Salt Lake (in our case this journey followed two beautiful days in Salt Lake City where we went one afternoon to Temple Square and noticed—because I am miserably? mercifully? shamefully? *physically incapable* of *not* noticing these sorts of dynamics any longer—that as we wandered the majestic halls of the museum, a museum which culminates at the top of a spiral incline in a striking bright white talking Jesus, that while all of the tour guides were very lovely, very young women, it appeared as if the entire population of current prophets, whom we encountered in a series of gold-framed professional headshots at the end of one exhibit, were elderly white men with white hair and striped ties, and although I find the comparatively contemporary origins of the religion and the—oft-repeated by the young women we passed—belief that according to the gospel a Mormon

family *will be together forever in the celestial kingdom* deeply enchanting I am no longer—at this age? with these experiences?—able to accept the seemingly obvious though under-ac-
knowledged reality that there is no adequate role for women in
most organized religions, that their mythologies, hierarchies,
and power structures are firmly and transparently sexist, that
the patriarchy erases, and that religion is frequently the enemy
of feminism . . .) and then follow the signs to the Golden Spike
National Historic Site where the Union and Central Pacific
Railroads were joined in 1869 creating a transcontinental route
that reduced coast-to-coast travel times in the United States
from several months to less than a week. Once past the visitor's
center, complete with replica steam-fueled locomotives and
scheduled reenactments of "the driving of the last spike," one
can proceed by weaving along an arid gravel path past old oil
jetties, salt flats, dust billows, cattle guards and barbwire fences,
blackbrush and desert sage, waterfowl, hovering shorebirds,
and into swarms of crickets and iridescent insects all the while
negotiating sharp bends under silver clouds for something like
ten miles until reaching a clearing and Spiral Jetty. Everything
looked bleached to us although the marble plaque that loomed
just above the bluff, a recent Eagle Scout project, said that
"Spiral Jetty is now largely white against pink due to salt en-
crustation," and according to the official Dia website one is
only able to see the piece during those months when water
levels are low enough, a detail O. had thought to check before
we left the hotel room. We scrambled down a tapered trail
through loose stones and weeds to where the rocks stretch out
levitating above sparkling salt flats. The day was hot. A small
tour bus of retirees got out behind us and poked their way

down the path, openly baffled by the minimalism. It's challenging to explain how a gigantic pile of rubble is so affecting but perhaps, I thought as we walked along the edges, it had to do with the way the jetty indicates perpetuity while concurrently forecasting its own inevitable decay among the wild wind and weather of rural Utah. Smithson (who was born in New Jersey and whose childhood doctor was, oddly, William Carlos Williams) discussed in interviews his interest in the idea of entropy, or "energy-drain," saying that it "contradicts the usual notion of a mechanistic world view," and that "it's a condition that's irreversible . . . a condition that's moving towards a gradual equilibrium," equilibrium being for Smithson the sweeping sameness of the charred post-apocalyptic universe, making even those shapes that have eternal potential most authentic when forsaken to their own known natural finale. In the late 1960s, when Smithson was searching for an ideal "site-nonsite" on which to make new work, he was struck by the Great Salt Lake, the fourth largest "terminal" lake in the world (meaning there is no outgoing water flow), which looked to him like "the edge of the sun, a *boiling curve*, an explosion rising into a fiery prominence." This manic, menacing vision of the end of the world manifests throughout Smithson's journals and at another points he writes: "On the slopes of Rozel Point I closed my eyes, and the sun burned crimson through the lids. I opened them and the Great Salt Lake was bleeding scarlet streaks. My sight was saturated by the color of red algae circulating in the heart of the lake, pumping into ruby currents, no they were veins and arteries sucking up the obscure sediments. My eyes became combustion chambers churning orbs of blood blazing by the light of the sun . . . Perception was heaving, the stomach turning. I was on a geologic fault that groaned within me . . . Surely, the storm clouds massing would turn into a rain of blood." The morning I saw Spiral Jetty—under a scorching sun which illuminated the iridescent salt-sand crystals in such a way as to evoke an ice-scape ("ice ages exist, ice ages exist") instead of reflecting the record-breaking heat wave that had

ignited fires up and down the parks and forests of the west coast—it was easy to imagine how Smithson could have entertained such a hallucination in this location. I would recall Smithson's vision later in the summer after reading an article by Kathryn Schulz in *The New Yorker* describing the pending peril of the Cascadia subduction zone, a fault line predicted to shift under Oregon and Washington creating the most massive catastrophic natural disaster the United States will ever see ("When the Cascadia earthquake begins," Schulz writes, "there will be . . . a cacophony of barking dogs and a long, suspended, what-was-that moment before the surface waves arrive.") It is thought that when the tectonic plates move there will be only moments before houses slide off their foundations, buildings collapse, and much of whole cities' infrastructures crumble to the ground; only the animals will know what terror is to beset them, as well as, of course, all those who have cautioned us. But that day, as I stared at Smithson's spiral of stones, which appeared more and more like an ominous warning from generations past, and as I watched our little dog do a dance when his paws got hot, I vaguely remembered, as perhaps others more definitively do, the now-absurd childhood fear that one day an *animated* (what cartoon does this image come from?) snake with evil powers would confront me with his gigantic pupils spinning *around and around and around and around and around* at increasing speeds until, if I wasn't vigilant, I would stare deep enough or long enough at the whirling optical coils that my body would become locked in the inescapable prison of hypnotism, losing all autonomy. Perhaps this cartoon snake was meant to demonstrate the ways in which staring is dangerous or, more probably I realize now, to teach the potential threat of a stranger's spellbinding suggestion. Hypnotism, both invoked and symbolized by a spiral, was once thought to censor one's memory of the very experience of being hypnotized, hence the well-known scene in which an ordinary citizen called to the stage can be made to squawk like a chicken (chickens being the perfect animal to imitate as they are legitimately transfixed by a line in the dirt) without any knowledge of having done so. There is the famous case of Dr. Franz Mesmer, an early proponent of psychological suggestion from whom the term "mesmerize" arrives, who in the 1770s transformed hypnotism from an occult practice to a "science" and apparently cured via cutting-edge hypnotic techniques the blindness of a young concert pianist, Maria Theresa Paradis. According to one source I read on the subject, when Maria Theresa's parents arrived to collect the girl from an appointment she didn't wish to go home and a spectacle ensued: Theresa's mother slapped the girl, Mesmer defended her, and Theresa's father *drew a sword* in an attempt to retrieve his daughter. The incident, which caused a scandal, is responsible for the ruin of Mesmer's medical reputation as well as the return of Maria Theresa's blindness. It isn't difficult when wading through eighteenth-century medical testimony to grow distracted by the gendered aspects of early therapeutic dynamics as every case seems to include an older "professional" male doctor practicing his theories on a vulnerable or unwilling female patient (Freud's Dora, etc.). We can only imagine the courage it must have taken to submit to these early psychological examinations intended to expose one's deepest fears or wrench repressed memories to the surface for "expert" inspection. Contemporary hypnosis, on the other hand, concentrates on states of consciousness closer to what we think of as meditation but is still intended to restructure a patient's approach to their behavior. To be hypnotized is to be captured or caught, to be trapped under the (hopefully charitable) governance of another; it would be a mistake to underestimate the appeal of an outside force gently nudging one's desires forward. With this in mind I attempted one afternoon after we had reached our final destination, O.'s childhood home of Port Townsend, to follow an instructional video I found on YouTube promising to teach the art of self-hypnotization. The video began by asking the listener to take three long, slow, soothing breaths, which I did self-consciously as a mellow-toned man with the voice of a cartoon villain murmured, "In this sweet mindless bliss . . . focus on my words and my words only . . . *breathe in . . . breathe out . . . breathe in . . . breathe out . . . breathe in . . . breathe out . . .*" and I tried to release any lingering tension accordingly. As someone untrained in meditation, terrible at relaxing, and generally resistant to authority, it is not surprising that I made a dreadful subject for this sort of experiment despite a desire for experiential research. I followed the instructions exactly but ultimately failed to feel as altered as I had hoped. Perhaps it's true that after staring long enough at the black-and-white spiral on the screen I felt a bit sleepy? Or possibly I was already too comfortable with the admonishing tones of my own internal counsel to succumb to suggestion? Should I get pregnant? The strangest part of that trip to Copenhagen, I realized, as I took several more deep breaths and set my gaze on the video's tacky spinning spiral, had occurred that very first night as we stumbled into the wet lilac light of dawn in the direction of the second "superior" dive bar and the young man I had just met, along with his friends, paused under a streetlamp and—apropos of nothing—serenaded us with the most beautiful, moving doowop rendition of "You're Nobody 'Til Somebody Loves You" that I'd ever heard and thus we learned that our acquaintances were members of a European boy band. Although my previous experiences have taught me that one must sometimes wait decades for a single astonishing moment to occur, I now know that occasionally, and only occasionally, they will arrive at once and in quick succession. I don't keep in touch with the Danish soprano but I'm still friends with a friend of his on Facebook who, according to photos, seems to have recently gotten married and had an adorable baby daughter.

# Sinkhole Suite

There was a bathtub in the kitchen. I shaved my legs while a
roommate sautéed spinach and D. perched shakily on the table,
his leather-booted feet tipping back a wooden chair while he
belted out songs from *Viva Last Blues*. This was Prague, early
2004. Bush was president and we were starting a war. Each
door in the communist-era apartment opened to the next,
forming a roiling circular river of flannel scarves, discolored
mugs, knit mittens, koruna, empty wine bottles, and firewood.
When you are young, there is the feeling of nothing to do;
some of us were in art school. Outside, we watched strangers
melt together under slate skies and a vague shadow of unrest.
I vowed to write for only others and spent a week composing
a term paper on Kafka's *The Trial*, earning an A-minus for one
of my comrades. We were always walking by the sausage stand
on the way to the castle. "Dobrý den!" we would crow when

entering the corner store. I had fled my home, Chicago, in a wild grief. Oil popped in the pan as the water drained.

•

The Space Out Competition, hosted annually in South Korea, determines who can do nothing for the longest—"nothing" being clearly defined: no sleeping, texting, meditating, or eating—the most specific of the most common acts. Participants "focus" on spacing out. Teenagers sit in a Seoul park slumped on lawn furniture with sun umbrellas and floppy hats; they languish on bright blue mats in such a way that a stranger could easily mistake the scene for a sleepy yoga class. Inspired by an overwhelming sense of productivity-oriented melancholy and excessive professional burn-out, WoopsYang, the event's creator, claimed that after much angst, an oppressive work schedule, and years of technology overload, "we would all feel better about doing nothing if we did nothing together as a group." There is a social component to the lack, as if to *not-do* should be a sponsored sport. According to an article in *Vice*, a broadcaster narrates the event and onlookers gawk at the proceedings from surrounding office buildings. WoopsYang says the idea of doing nothing is catching on, spreading slowly to other nations. Last year's winner, a local rapper, claims to have spent a fair amount of time practicing for the contest at home.

•

"I have nothing to say / and I am saying it," writes John Cage in "Lecture on Nothing," insisting that a work's strength depends upon its structure more than its message—that form must be sturdy enough to bear the wildness of unanticipated content. "Each moment / presents what happens," and therefore gives shape to improvisation, surprise. Locate the structure, Cage suggests in an essay composed of strict rhythms and careful mathematical measurements, and via its limits you will access an engine. In Cage's most famous musical piece, *4'33"*, musicians were instructed not to play their instruments for the totality of the orchestral composition resulting in what seemed at first like several minutes of silence but was later recognized as the symphonic ambient noise (and expressed frustration) of a clueless audience. Inspired by Robert Rauschenberg's *White Paintings*—blank white canvases all painted the same shade of white—Cage reveled in the intricacy and detail—the *meaning*—available in conceptual work, presumably causing his audience to wonder if there is truly such a thing as *nothing* or if the very idea creates a system, a hole, or a frame.

•

*He was a twinkle in your eye* is only an expression. *A thorn in your gut. A soul tornado. Late cargo. Snow.*

•

At P.'s Fourth of July barbecue in Chicago there are a million babies and one trembling, anxious good dog: mine. People eat cheddar brats, rosé Jell-O shots, play bags, and talk about Lake Life for Labor Day. K.'s hair is especially long and M. tells me that last week, on the El, she was nosily peering over a man's shoulder, reading his large phone's text in Spanish, first an article about a soccer game and then one on the latest damage caused by our misogynist demagogue of a president. She swore out loud in reaction to something she read and was caught in her snooping, resulting in a conversation with this stranger. After a long, polite series of questions, M. and the man on the El realized that they knew several of the same people and, in fact, were most likely cousins.

•

When the woman was young, maybe three or four, her mother was the director of a Montessori school to which she went daily. She remembers singing songs, playing with blocks, and standing in a long line for a long time. She remembers perforating a gigantic, table-sized map of the globe, continent by continent, country by country, having been given a single pushpin. She remembers the fuzzy edges of the construction paper and working diligently, for what seemed like an eternity, with what is now a familiar combination of pride and despair. Was this what her whole life would be like? The woman's husband, she later found out, also attended Montessori school as a child—his in Washington, hers in Wisconsin, both in the early eighties—and his chief memory of that time is the moment his teacher asked him to blow his nose and he realized that instead he could simply suck the snot back into his head.

•

"The Escalade went wham," explains the man interviewed for the story, "and the power line went, like, pow." You click on the picture. An article in the *Milwaukee Journal Sentinel* reports on—among other consequences of recently troubling weather patterns—a twenty-by-thirty-foot sinkhole that broke open on the corner of North and Oakland. It's 2010; the emergency is just down the street and this is the second of three sinkholes that have opened within a mile of your home since you moved here three years ago. According to the story, around 8 p.m. on July 22 a man named Mark Pawlik was walking along North Street near the large and muddy scar of the Pizza Man Restaurant, which had recently burned down, and saw the top of a streetlight jutting diagonally out of the asphalt. He leaned over the hole. A car had broken through the road and dropped straight down into the gaping mouth of the ground. It had been storming all summer. Pawlik was able to assist the owner of the Escalade out of the pit and the driver survived uninjured. You zoom in on the image. Taken from somebody's phone it shows the top of a black truck surrounded by broken hunks of cement and the clumped dirt of the cracked earth. The incident is reported as a man-saves-man miracle with little inquiry into what might have caused it. There is no description of the horror of the street's collapse and only one sentence noting the disturbing fact that the car was left running—still lodged in the depression—two days later. Imagine waiting patiently at a red light for the earth to become your sudden tomb.

•

Doing nothing is often the reward for having everything. If you are born into nothing you are regularly required to *do more* and *give more* and *feel worse* as a sort of cost to the journey of surviving. Very few people do nothing *and* want nothing. If you are accustomed to doing nothing from the beginning of your life, say, because someone else is doing the things you should be doing for you, you might be asked to do something for a while, to prove that you can, that you are capable, and then, in celebration of doing anything at all, you are allowed to do nothing else forever. For some, the consequence of doing something competently, let alone well, is to be repeatedly tasked with doing everything for everyone forever. It is still true that if you identify as what is called a man quite often after having done very little you may relax and do no more, at least until you feel ready.

•

Lorine Niedecker: "I'm pillowed and padded, pale and puffing / lifting household stuffing—/ carpets, dishes / benches, fishes / I've spent my life in nothing."

•

You read about a man who was silent for seventeen years. One day, in his late twenties, John Francis simply stopped speaking; at first he saw the gesture as a silly expression of sincerity toward his girlfriend and later he came to understand his silence as a type of protest; to remove his speech from the world would open up space—space for others and space for listening. During the years that he was silent Francis walked everywhere, often hundreds of miles in one direction. Doing nothing, or as close to nothing as possible, can be a kind of activism. Don't speak, don't touch, don't disturb or deplete energy. Today, the president has withdrawn our nation from the Paris Accord, which many consider a vital step toward addressing global climate change. Ice caps are melting. Sea levels are rising. Coral is over. In Roy Scranton's *Learning to Die in the Anthropocene*, he argues that humans can and should still attempt to make meaning of our lives even, or especially, in the face of inevitable global upheaval, certain demise. He says we must learn how to transition together into an uncertain future, a future with food riots, damaged infrastructure, and terminal temperatures. Knowing that death is not optional but inevitable (or more accurately, as Scranton clarifies, already done) he insists that our greatest human questions are still in front of us as we speed rapidly toward our species' finale.

•

This baby I'm looking at on my phone sees nothing, says nothing, understands nothing—he's a mass of bubbly gurgles and excrement. This baby who I'm looking at on my phone is a new baby, *fresh*, dressed in blue with petite ankles and wise eyes. He's my brother's child, named after my father. He concentrates on what is most critical: warmth, skin, Mom, fear. He represents more than he apprehends, born an echo. Next is a picture of my niece, E., who is extremely interested in the dog bowl. E. sleeps with a white noise machine meant to resemble the sounds of nothing, which for her are the muted booms of the forgotten womb.

•

This afternoon, at an artist's residency, over lunch, a fellow writer and I mull over how many times one can use the word "the" to introduce nouns in a list. A musician unzips her harp and we speak of chance. Later, at a picnic, a painter tells me that when he was young his mother would hand-stitch thick notebooks from special paper, encouraging him to fill them with drawings. One resident shows us photos of her looms, which were brought all the way to the Headlands, via U-Haul, on the first day, their pieces disassembled and wrapped. She explains that the loom limbs have creaky joints, individual proclivities and leans, like any body, and that her craft depends upon the material and the place: weaving as action, as the composition of a text—not simply resolving a pattern. The place where we reside is quiet. We wake early, as the sun rises, and work in silence. It smells like pine and eucalyptus. The closer we get to a sense of nothing the more likely an *awareness* will emerge. I am too relaxed to nap. M. makes a full body suit of hay and walks into the tall grass. D. has us aim mirrors at the sun's rays. A lovely British intern tells me that in Wales they call microwaves *pop de pings*. The fading paint on the harp, we are told by the harpist, has been shaded with a sharpie.

•

Let us head nowhere together—knowing nothing—palm in palm, a blessing.

•

Items that have been swallowed by the earth: a pickup truck, a hotel, a yard, a man while he slept in his own bed, a campsite, a town, a church, a road, someone's uncle's house, a big rig, the fourteenth hole of an Illinois golf course, a housing complex in China, a three-story building in Guatemala, oil field equipment, trees, mushrooms, a tar pit, a water department van, an entire Oklahoma ghost town, fields, sidewalks, poles, street signs, tourists, sewers, trash.

·

A car crashed into another car, underwater. My childhood neighbor, Mrs. J., told us this story. Apparently, this occurred "up north," meaning, in my youth, Wisconsin. A father and his two sons were heading out to ice fish when the weight of their truck split the frozen surface of the lake; they leapt out of the car in time to save themselves, but the vehicle dropped through the floes of broken ice and sank. The following summer, when the family paid to have the truck towed out of the lake, Mrs. J. said that divers discovered the vehicle had gone down slowly and at a gradual diagonal at which point it crashed head-on into another car that had dropped in the exact same spot a few winters earlier, now jammed in the mucky bottom, facing up. One of the owners sued the other, I think, but who can recall?

·

Everywhere the woman looked there was something that used to be something else. She lived in Cleveland, between an abandoned elementary school, an abandoned Walmart, an abandoned movie theater, an abandoned country club, and not far from an abandoned celestial observatory. Children roamed the streets alone, unsupervised for hours. Once she saw a five-year-old boy in a suit accompanied by a five-year-old girl in a lacy long dress pushing an infant down the street in its carriage, sans adult. When you are new, it is easier to ascertain the qualities a place enjoys about itself; one doesn't excuse uniqueness with context. Here, there were flowers growing through tree stumps. No one scooped their stoop and citizens could be spotted walking down the center of the street with a middle finger to traffic. There were vacant houses, a waning population, and problems with teen suicide. Despite what locals would say, there were no decent tacos. It was not a peaceful place, the woman thought. It could be pretty. The building she worked in was filled with asbestos. People were generally friendly.

•

We fly a long way to see friends. They tell us about the history of their furniture. The chairs are positioned at odd angles. It is good to be together again among the tall trees, imagining novels.

•

*Am I not working hard enough to decide?* It is clear to everyone, including me, that I am doing nothing about an action that must be chosen. Meanwhile my body grows older. I desire each outcome completely. How can one listen to a void? Must I erase all other thoughts in order to have this one?

•

In Prague we ate fried cheese sandwiches while walking from one apartment to another. I wore long knit sweaters and dresses over pants. Photos disclose my dirty hair. What else is there to remember? We frequented the Marquis de Sade. On a trip to a friend's cabin in the woods of Slovakia we sipped his father's homemade moonshine. There was tea and music, long walks in the park. I remember a painting at the National Gallery: three boxes—or was it three birds?—hand drawn in ink, plain and thick. I couldn't tell you exactly what it looked like but the lines have lived in me as a feeling ever since.

·

When a person is writing they might appear to the outside observer as if they are doing nothing. A few flicks of the wrist, scribbles, ticks. When they are reading, even more so. Both occupations suggest a trance state, a white heat, the overwhelming presence of the overmind. This is why when you are truly making a work of art *distraction hurts*; it pains the maker by shuttling them to the surface, forcing them back into their own self. Once they have been yanked from that other place (which is, of course, technically *nowhere*) it can be impossible to return, a heartbreak.

·

King Lear: "Nothing will come of nothing. Speak again."

·

H. and I missed the Memorial Day party because of feminism. It was important to review the minutiae, to convince each other that despite such audacious affronts our boundaries would only become clearer. She was visiting for the weekend. The matter at hand, in this case, was the gender dynamic in my new job and a particularly condescending interaction H. had had with a male acquaintance who desired the sort of exhausting attention that could only be described as *concern trolling*. We sat on the porch with our pamplemousse. I told her O. had proposed while I was researching Cleopatra, attempting to determine whether or not she had died of an asp bite, as I'd always heard, or if her handmaidens had smuggled poison into the room, after which one of them—so the most famous painting of the instant illustrates—took her own life with the remains of the potion. H. relayed a story in which Cleopatra, who had been banished from Alexandria by her brother (*also her husband*, said H., and their parents were married too, such that the siblings had only one set of grandparents!), snuck back into the city rolled up in a rug to be unfurled at the feet of Caesar. The sun was sinking. Large questions remained. Should she move to Jerusalem? If I quit now, would I work again? Satchel scooted near, licking her knee's open wound. Do you have a legal pad? asked H. Let's write some things down.

•

At the residency we actively practice doing nothing. It's harder than it looks, but very satisfying. There's no cell phone service and only infrequent access to the internet. I stop reading the news. I stop talking to my friends and family. Sometimes I stare for long moments at nothing, others I focus on the wall. Everywhere I turn I have nothing to do. I miss the dog. The patterns in the rug are redundant. I return to the window. In a natural setting, I find that every shape resembles a deer. I try to remember what it is I have been doing with my life until this point... Was it meaningful; was it clear?

•

To séance means to sit; it is a session, a time of rest and receiving. If all goes well, a conversation occurs. The body is a conduit, a form through which communication cannot be predicted. To séance is to wait, to expect, to prepare, and to encourage contact. The surrounding spirits—bodiless, indistinct—are content. They have been doing nothing longer than you have. Years of your life spent thinking you wanted to be somewhere else, do something else, feel some other way—ambition, privilege, desperation, or ennui?

•

Cage: "If anybody is sleepy / let him go to sleep."

•

Rumor has it that in the sixties or seventies there were preserved dead bodies at the bottom of Lake Tahoe. Jacques Cousteau supposedly submerged himself in the lake only to find a world of pickled corpses buried in the frozen muck. "The world isn't ready for the horrors I have seen," he was quoted as having said upon surfacing. It has long been alleged that what can be found underwater is a greater mystery even than that which exists in outer space.

•

But you and I aren't in the same room. I would leave this blank if I could listen to you laugh at me.

•

In Edgar Allan Poe's "A Premature Burial," the narrator describes the sense of rigidity in his muscles, the slowed-down heartbeat and shallow inhalations that accompanied what the doctors then diagnosed as "catalepsy." It is a nervous condition—real or imagined—that creates an intense paranoia of being buried alive. "My nerves became thoroughly unstrung," said Poe's narrator, "and I fell a prey to perpetual horror. I hesitated to ride, or to walk, or to indulge in any exercise that would carry me from home. In fact I no longer dared trust myself out of the immediate presence of those who were aware of my proneness . . . lest, falling into one of my fits, I should be buried before my real condition could be ascertained."

•

It can't possibly matter what comes next, I think, in an instant of foolish optimism. Nothing means anything! We're advancing rapidly into the abyss. I catch the smell of summer mulch. Any minute now the limits of life will demand that I shower and go to the grocery store.

•

A sinkhole occurs when air gets into the gaps of the ground and the pressure pushes matter back. Water shifts and erodes, veins fill with moisture, roots reroute. To create nothing out of something: the mechanics of a pocket. Under tar and potholes roads figure rivulets of their own disruption and whole miles of lines crack wide open. They can create a void the size of a house—an ordinary recession. The opening of a thinly covered depression is a terrible burial. Beware. A pocket of oxygen will leak. Shallow gasps will kill you. Breathing is futile. Silence travels.

# What Remains To Be Seen

There were thirty extra-long multicolored helium toy balloons at little L.'s birthday party. He was turning one, my brother's son, and proving to be an excellent drummer. The balloons were surprisingly strong, and partway through the party someone knotted a few ribboned ends around the waist of an empty Old Style, which levitated in the kitchen's center for the remainder of the day. Two small cakes sat on the stove, neither meant to be eaten. One was a melting pastel blob, abandoned for its irregular shape, and the second stood similar in size but with straighter sides and a bouquet of turquoise and lavender balloons hand-iced on top. Neither cake had egg in it; L. was allergic. The idea was for him to grab this scaled dessert with his miniature manic hands and smash it—smearing frosting as we watched—and for us to take photos that, presumably, he'd glance at decades later with a saccharine surge of nostalgia for a performance he couldn't recall, this image representing the burgeoning start of his selfhood (or his parents' sense of his selfhood), which, by the time he would think to consider this evidence, would have begun to drift and complicate. As I sat on the arm of the couch, a cheese curd in hand, staring at the floating tin beer can, I was reminded of the photo of a proposed performance piece in which the tethered ties of four enormous gold pig balloons were to be anchored on the Chicago River in such a way and at such an angle as to block, for a brief but relieving period of time, our current president's name from casting its rancid pall upon the city. It was spring 2018; I was visiting Chicago from Cleveland. The morning before, I had wandered from my mother's apartment in the South Loop up Michigan Avenue, past Grant Park and the Art Institute, over the river and through mobs of late-spring shoppers to check out the Howardena Pindell exhibit *What Remains to Be Seen* at the Museum of Contemporary Art, where a major survey of her work was being shown for the first time in her fifty-year career. I had read a bit about Pindell and was primarily there to see her 1980 short film, *Free, White and 21*, in which she delivers a twelve-minute monologue recounting her lifelong experiences of racism while slowly wrapping a gauze bandage around her head and—via quick interspersed clips of herself in whiteface—interrupting this narrative with pity, condescension, and suspicion as the character of a falsely concerned white woman. In one story, Pindell describes how her kindergarten teacher tied her to a cot with a sheet when she asked to go to the bathroom during naptime. In another, she explains how her name was removed from a student government ballot in college because she was Black and, therefore, "inappropriate for [the] office." Pindell, in cat-eye sunglasses, heavy ivory foundation, and a blonde wig, replies to the anecdotes with lines such as, "You ungrateful little . . . You know, you really must be paranoid. Those things never happened to me." *Free, White and 21*—whose title references a phrase initially uttered by voting men in the 1820s, reiterated ad nauseam in midcentury Hollywood movies to underscore the casual privileges of white youth—marks the first moment that Pindell, thirty-seven and already an established artist, publicly addressed race and racism in her work in an attempt, she said, to tackle the art-world tokenism she had endured for years. Pindell made the video shortly after she went from working at the Museum of Modern Art to teaching at SUNY Stony Brook, where in the first month of the job she was in a car accident that resulted in head trauma and partial amnesia, motivating the use of video as a method of reclaiming memories, including those of her so-called feminist friends disregarding discussions of race as part of their activism. Toward the end of the film—after Pindell has mummified herself by wrapping a bandage around her head, covering her surface with the same material one would use to staunch an open wound—she peels a layer of fake translucent skin off her face. Still in the guise of a white woman, she pulls a pale stocking over her head, underscoring the relentlessness of the masks she's expected to wear, the layers of invisibility she's been forced to perform. Previously known for abstract material-focused color studies, Pindell, after filming *Free, White and 21*, began making autobiographical paintings: large canvases covered with narrative scraps from travel and research, family photos, stitched symbols of her ancestry and African heritage. She turned from what some would call "pure" painting—a process-oriented approach interested in material, craft, lyricism, and intuition—to a clearer narrative style, one integrating shards of association, inquiry, and documentation that trouble the overlap of the personal and political. When *Free, White and 21* ended, I wandered into the bright ivory gallery where Pindell's earlier paintings were arranged and saw what looked, from a short distance, like panels of scattered crayon bottoms or a speckled subsection of a rave's floor. (Would little L. know what a rave was? Had the world already shifted thus?) Moving closer, I noticed thousands of multicolored perfect circles the size of a pinkie's tip arranged in great piles onto unframed stretched canvases creating a liquid, jubilant, multitextured field suggestive, perhaps, of a shag rug, speckled wall, or foamy shoreside ocean swell. Pindell's crumblike rainbow chads (the result, it turned out, of a hole punch) formed constellations; swirling eddies of pigment and dye; mysterious brightnesses popping through hues of contrasting shades. Some of the paintings were a potpourri of pixels, while others read as subtle geometrically inspired color studies reminiscent of Agnes Martin or Mark Rothko—fading in shade as they progressed across the plane, fluctuating in tone and mood, surprising with moments of delicate difference or balanced variation. One might want to touch these ragged three-dimensional fields; I didn't touch them. The paintings developed an interesting tension between a mechanical, automated compositional approach and the chaos of handmade, abstract outcomes. In the exhibition material, Naomi Beckwith wrote, "Pindell's innovation is to invest the object with a sense of gesture and bodily movement sans the outsized heroic antics of expressionism," separating her mode of physical composition from the more dramatic (male) artists of the preceding generation—Jackson Pollock, Wassily Kandinsky—and instead conversing with the grounded, earth-based performative practices of her peers Ana Mendieta and Cecilia Vicuña. These abstract paintings focused on style over story, material over image, and action over outcome, and as so often happens, it turned out to be the unknown, unexpected work that would disturb my psyche—as if discombobulation was the architect of retention—just as how one recalls the moment they were lost more sharply than the miles in which they knew where they were headed, consciousness progressing in an only occasionally punctured daze. Pindell's hole punches were on my mind the following afternoon; between pushing the birthday baby in his plastic car and refilling my rosé, I scrolled through my phone to catch again an image of *Untitled* (1975), which, when held up, created a sudden funny tableau of backlit polka dots hovering on a screen in front of the real-life helium balloons that were sailing softly past the windows in the late sun. The piece I'd taken a snapshot of (was I allowed to do that?) had a yellow backdrop with circles of blue clumped and spread along with white and red, the colors combining in such a way as to recall the plastic-blue palette of Tan Zi Xi's *Plastic Ocean*, a space-based sculpture in which pieces of trash are strung from a gallery's ceiling to create a dense, concave hanging pile of sea garbage intended to represent the overwhelming amount of crap currently clogging the world's oceans. In pictures of *Plastic Ocean*, visitors peer upward at layers of trash like I imagine a contemporary fish might or, perhaps, like a guest at a more accurately representative aquarium—constellations of waste blocking light from piercing the tank's briny fathoms. I had plastic on my mind;

these were frightening times. A few weeks after little L.'s birthday party, as the humid Lake Erie air first challenged my
breathing and each square of sidewalk grew rife with the inde-
cipherable prelinguistic chalky warning signs of neighborhood
children, I sought relief from the Cleveland heat in a trip to see
O. out east, where he was driving research vessels for a marine
lab six miles off of Maine's coast. It had been nearly five years
since we'd moved to Ohio for my job, which had since proved
a stable but frustrating obstacle to life outside an eigh-
teenth-floor English department located in a towering Brutal-
ist building with skinny sniper windows and the amusing lore
of nineteenth-floor flooding and loose asbestos. The island
promised, O. said, cool Atlantic winds, lawless gulls, and "no
one you know." I'd had a strange few years; through a series of
bureaucratic mishandlings, I'd absorbed the workload of multiple academic positions, which, because the situation couldn't be
swiftly fixed, was masked by a parade of well-meaning compli-
ments from colleagues intending to keep my spirits up: "You
seem so *sane*," someone would say, or "Keep smiling!" and
"You're just doing this work *too well* for help." Perhaps I should
have recognized something was afoot when the offer letter was
mysteriously addressed to someone named "Hope," or when I
was repeatedly confused for a person named "Emily," as if my
very presence evoked the ghosts of women past, floating and
transposable. My experiences felt as if they belonged to another time and place: being counseled not to have children; an
earnest inquiry about the quality of my handwriting; or the
repeated suggestion that I handle students via methods of
"punishment" and "discipline." The more time I spent in the
tower, the farther I felt from the world, and so it was one

Tuesday morning that while our neighbor paced back and forth fertilizing his lawn and friends settled in for a summer of sprinklers and bug spray, I packed a few bags and drove east with the dog. Somehow it's only in retrospect that I can recognize how badly I needed a break, and as we rushed eastward up I-90, past the cracked roofs of roadside barns and truck-backs singing "VETS BEFORE REFUGEES" or "KASICH FOR US," I experienced a sensation similar to that of a heated helmet of lead levitating from my head, or several suffocating clutches relaxing their grip, but perhaps it was merely my own numb heart beating again, generating the type of strident interior buoyancy that signifies freedom (free-*dom*, free-*dom*, free-*dom*) and only ever temporarily interrupts the perpetual panic of adulthood. As I drove through the first of the tolls, I recalled an experience on another road trip two years ago when I dropped down to Washington, D.C. for a few days before heading to D.'s wedding in Baltimore, and had wandered into the National Museum of Women in the Arts, a place I had never been but, based on a bus-stop vestibule's billboard, was curious about. This was June 2016, and I had made the mistake of rereading something I had written years ago in which the narrator recognizes her own internal vision via the expression of a woman being photographed strolling down the street in Chicago, a photograph I had encountered for the first time in our nation's capital. I believed, perhaps foolishly, that if I returned to the source I might resurrect a bit of magic. That day I was greeted in the museum's rose-marbled lobby by an animated Russian docent who unnecessarily apologized for her imperfect English before inundating me with information concerning new exhibits, galleries, and the history of the

building. She pointed to a life-sized painting behind her as she described the founder, Wilhelmina Cole Holladay, who had installed the collection in 1983 in a formidable former Masonic temple. The docent suggested that I not skip the third floor—"Many people miss the third floor," she said—and in her opinion it was, though considerably smaller, the most significant. I walked up the three sets of stairs and saw, around the first corner, a large photograph depicting about a dozen female high-school students leaning over and against the sides of a speedboat, spray and waves shooting up, the girls laughing, their faces wide with outdoor smiles and the sort of awe caused only by flying. In the back of the evergreen boat, on the right side of the photograph, an adult man steered the engine—a *Mariner*, so it was labeled—and grinned at the horizon, gripping a large Palestinian flag. I considered the way the girls' bodies must have felt: airy, aloft, blazing. A long row of buildings lined the coast, contrasting in their ivory brightness the coal navy of the sea as well as the white hijabs of the girls, which coursed against their black robes. Based on the angle of the photograph, I guessed that Tanya Habjouqa, the artist, was perched on another boat, one zooming parallel to the first. The caption mentioned that the girls and their chauffer were not permitted to steer more than six miles off the coast, beyond which was considered Israeli territory—the water forming an invisible wall around a dozen teens forever caught blinking into the sea's sun, reveling in their five-minute cruise. I kept walking. On another floor, a Jenny Holzer piece screamed, "RAISE BOYS AND GIRLS THE SAME," and as I drifted through a series of bright photographs by Rania Matar called *A Girl and Her Room*, which depicted the bedrooms of

American and Lebanese teenage girls—replete with messy beds, lipstick tubes, records, and celebrity posters—I considered how crucial place is to our identity-forming narratives. This particular exhibit seemed to be asking who in this world is allowed to leave home and who can travel safely. I could, I knew, and I couldn't. I wondered about the docent, what she had found on the third floor and what she had thought I'd take an interest in; I was the only person in the museum. A week later I would awake at three in the morning in a hotel room to the sounds of pounding on a neighboring door. "Let me in!" screamed a man, beating faster, louder, then to a new rhythm. "*Let! Me! The! Fuck! In!*" A pause. Still half asleep I flipped over on my pillow, wondering if I should dial the front desk, wondering if someone already had. The pounding quieted after a minute, and I could pick out a soft voice (a manager? The person in the room?) whispering something unintelligible. Finally, passing my door on his way to the elevator, the man yelled loudly to the walls and all who were listening on the other sides of them: "That fucking cunt! That goddamn fucking *cunt*. I'm going to kill her!" The following morning a father and son sat adjacent to me in a café. I was reading *Speedboat*; we were all eating eggs. I overheard the father asking his high-school-age son to describe a few of the girls who had been at the graduation party they had presumably attended the evening before. The son started in about who had been in what class, who played what sport. The father interrupted: "What was that *one*? With the shirt on? . . . Is it Rachel?" The son nodded, chewing bacon. "I thought so. I sure did like the look of that one." Maybe I so clearly recalled these specific incidents because they occurred during a short period of time, the summer of 2016, in which I imagined the attitude toward gender equality in America was changing. It wasn't. One morning after I finally arrived on O.'s island, which included swarms of biology students, environmental photographers, marine faculty, bird-banders, gull-speckled staff housing, and a famous nineteenth-century poet's elegantly replicated garden, I walked over to the rust-colored concrete observation tower and watched as O. and his colleagues put together what looked like a giant steel torpedo intended to drag an underwater net in such a way that the island's interns could collect samples of sea scum. As I wandered through the adjacent laboratory, peering at decades-old aquatic skeletons and sea fetuses floating in oily preservative, I spotted, taped to the sun-worn lab door, a single sheet of loose-leaf that announced the following evening's lecture, "Plastics and the Anthropocene," reminding me of the most recent issue of *National Geographic*, which featured a dozen striking photographs of ocean animals encumbered by plastic. The most adorable of these unsettling shots was a small amber seahorse dragging a pastel-pink Q-tip along the bottom of the turquoise sea with its curlicue tail. Another photo showed a pack of Ethiopian hyenas nosing through piles of trash, and a third caught an Australian sponge crab wearing a transparent cape of plastic instead of its rightful opaque shell, which would have protected it from predators. Even the deepest floors of the ocean had been tainted by toxic debris: grocery bags, pill bottles, straws, coffee holders, microbeads, tarps, tape, car parts, bottle caps, jacket fibers, carry-out containers, shoes, ghost nets, children's toys, mattress stuffing, lost balloons, cutlery, shampoo bottles, pylons, oil jugs, and so on. Soap was turning up in the stomachs of turtles, lead circulated in the bloodstreams of Midwestern children, opioids were detected in Puget Sound's mussels, and evidence of Fukushima's nuclear signature could be found in California wines. For years biologists had been studying tern populations on the tiny island next to O.'s, he told me, and each summer three scientists protected the breeding population from predators by living as unobtrusively as possible among thousands of birds in a small cabin with solar electricity, a guard dog, and no running water. There were common, roseate, and arctic terns on the island, many of which would travel more than forty thousand miles for the winter, migrating along the east coast to South America, taking about a month to commute in the fall and just two weeks for their trip back to Maine. For close to two decades they had returned to this island, where the biologists monitored the birds' health, studied patterns in mating and flight, and, more recently, tracked the number of plastic bags the terns were ingesting. One of their concerns, beyond this new evidence of pollution, was the phenomenon of "dread flight," which is when an entire colony, suddenly scared of a predator, grows absolutely silent for a few minutes, and then abruptly ascends en masse, never to return to the same home again. The biologists did their best to ensure conditions were hospitable but worried that one year their subjects would disappear in an instant. Even in the ornithological world, it seemed, the power of a single arbitrary bully could spook an entire population, changing the course of history for generations. But here is the point: before the summer started; before little L.'s birthday party in Chicago and the trip out east; before I settled into a new academic year, a new overpriced parking pass, student poems, book edits, lunchtime peanut-butter sandwiches, trash days, snow shoveling, and utility bills; before a myriad of personal diversions and the daily drive through the strange and mostly vacant strip of land between uptown and downtown Cleveland called "Midtown," with its public service billboards ("Syphilis is Serious," "Not Ready: Use a Condom"), tall weeds, hospital construction, and old Dennis Kucinich signs, I encountered a video about the city in which I lived that would stay with me for years and, in time, come to summarize my feelings about the place more clearly than any personal insight. It wasn't the "Hastily Made Cleveland Tourism Video" or "Believeland"; this short documentary, which I first discovered via the *Cleveland Scene*, exhibited something specific about *Rust Belt culture*, a questionable term that was being used ad nauseam by journalists that year, and that itself seemed a misunderstanding of the misunderstandings of the misunderstood, and at the same time the key to some larger national truth, one that was only beginning to manifest. The video was called "Balloonfest" and took place during two days in 1986. It was made by a cinematographer from Missouri named Nathan Truesdell, who claimed he first learned of the Cleveland event from a nurse. Apparently, Truesdell was watching an instructional video on how to shape balloon animals—practicing for his application to clown college—when he tripped over a coffee table and broke both his arms. The subsequent documentary, which Truesdell originally intended to be feature-length, was—after years of experimenting with interviews, reporting, and oral storytelling—narrowed down to a six-and-a-half-minute collage of thirty-year-old footage gathered from the Northeast Ohio Broadcast Archives, WJW Cleveland, and resident home videos. It begins with a broom-mustached newscaster excitedly interviewing Los Angeles–based balloon artist Treb Heining with a thin silver microphone in sunny downtown Cleveland. After Heining predicts that a child can fill "two to three balloons a minute," the viewers are returned to the studio, where an energetic blonde and her partner report on a live feed showing—in the warm, washed-out tones of eighties TV lens colors—citizens milling about in large sunglasses, striped polos, big jeans, crop tops, and (still) the subtlest of bell-bottoms. The city of Cleveland, in collaboration with the local branch of UNICEF, was attempting to break the world record for a simultaneous balloon launch, sending more than 1.5 million balloons into the ether in one release to beat the previous record held by Disneyland. The fervor for this ludicrous feat was undeniable; footage shows thousands of citizens gathered in a historically dead downtown to pump plastic pockets full of gas and gently float the orbs into a three-story-high mesh fishing net, which caught the bits of latex flyers in a single spot so they could be released into the pure skies all together. What an optimistic vision this must have been. In the video, commentators are nearly hysterical with praise for this celebratory image of change, overeagerly boosting a city that for as long as anyone can remember has been associated with an almost-spiritual losing streak. In one clip, Big Chuck (a local radio personality) interviews a distraught middle-aged woman named Mary Ann about her wristwatch, which she had tied to some balloons when the clasp popped open and the watch sailed away—"Has anyone seen it?"—after which Big Chuck mysteriously kisses this stranger on the lips. The cameraman focuses on children with sore-speckled, gauze-taped fingers earned from too much inflating. A Los Angeles spokesman for the event claims—with the earnestness of a child trying to garner interest in their lemonade stand—that he and his wife have "been in this city for six months" and have "even considered" moving to Cleveland despite their friends thinking they're crazy. The countdown begins, and as thousands of balloons are finally released into the air, an announcer cries: "*We* did it! . . . I wanna sing 'Up, Up and Away'! . . . There is no mistake on the lake anymore! Cleveland . . . home of the . . . home of the . . . home of the . . . Rock & Roll Hall of Fame!" The balloons rise and swirl higher than the city's skyscrapers, creating almost-aquatic eddies and organic, flowing flight patterns reminiscent of a murmur of birds or school of minnows. What comes next is sadly unsurprising: a storm stumbles over the horizon and the cold front immediately sinks whole swaths of the just-freed swarm. They blow every which way and then dip and land. It's instant chaos. The balloons become little bits of garbage docking in the wrong spots. Thousands of plastic pieces drift into already toxic Lake Erie, and others, so a news anchor exclaims in a clip from the following morning, have traveled in packs to Canada. The viewer learns that the ancient curse of Cleveland is still working, that the city didn't break the world record after all, and that the balloons, instead of cementing transformation, became swift harbingers of doom, spelling danger for sailors navigating the messy party favor of a lake. The following morning the Coast Guard was dispatched to search for two missing men who had gone overboard the previous night in their fishing boat. As the young captain says on tape, hair blowing in the wind, the hundreds of thousands of multicolored balloons bobbing on the surface of the waves made finding a flotation device or a human head considerably more difficult. The men's bodies washed ashore shortly after. On film, the environmental impact is never mentioned. One has the sense that this production, like a tiny cake meant to be smashed, was something intended for destruction—an act of willful decadence—but the truth is that in the 1980s the city of Cleveland badly wanted to make a national mark, and now, more than thirty years later, one can still feel that desperation, that desire in the air. I watched the video several times, returning not only for the humor of a stunt gone wrong but also for the splendor of the still shots. One clip shows hundreds of balloons drifting on the lake like confetti, reminding me not only of Yayoi Kusama's immersive, kaleidoscopic *Infinity Mirrors*—which I was to see later that summer at the Cleveland Museum of Art—but also of Howardena Pindell's polka dots in their speckled excellence. Perhaps the most startling visual moment in the documentary was when the balloons, just liberated from their net, slowly rose and congealed into one tail-like, gaseous, swirling figure, mirroring the tufts of nearby smokestacks. The colors of the balloons in this shot blended not, as one would guess, to brown or black, but instead to a striking rust against the clear sky, curling up and around Terminal Tower like fire, an orange omen of what would later become my generation's greatest nightmare. But no—that was impossible; no one in 1986 would imagine that planes would fly into skyscrapers, that buildings would buckle. It was not yet easy to believe that the end of the world, the end of memory, was upon us. What can we save, I wondered—and what's left to the wind? That which is intended for Cleveland can end up in Canada. That which keeps time might absent into autumn sky. The smiles on the faces in the film had a bit more time, but not a ton. They burned bright in a pathetic and flammable city submerged in the trash of its own sad party. *Let go*, one might think, of any other kind of future. *Let go. Let go. Let go.*

# The Crystal Corner

We spent the first weekend of our honeymoon in a charming but sparsely inhabited Lake Geneva resort before heading northwest through miles of Wisconsin farmland toward Madison where K. and I had both lived—me in college, him after grad school—and where we still regularly reminisced about nights spent with his wife, L., at the Crystal Corner, or weekends with their toddler-aged son, J., lounging with a pack of friends on the terrace of the Memorial Union. I had married O. in Milwaukee the Friday before and my friend K., who was on spring break, was looking for a nearby place to work on his novel, so we met up for a portion of the trip. After a few days of fish fry, cheese curds, brandy old fashioneds, and ramen (few of which could be found in my home of Cleveland) the three of us planned a visit to House on the Rock, a tourist spot about thirty miles west of town, known for its bizarre architecture, eccentric collections, and the world's largest indoor carousel. Both K. and O. had been there before—K., he said, fatefully, on his first date with L.—and O. with an ex-girlfriend. As we drove to the site, passing Frank Lloyd Wright's early 1900s Prairie School construction Taliesin—framed in the distance by other Wright-inspired knockoffs, as if his midcentury-modern aesthetic had infected Wisconsin's water—I remembered that this was the location where Wright's mistress Mamah Cheney (an early feminist and the wife of one of his clients) had been brutally murdered along with her two small children by a servant at Wright's new property. The servant, so the story goes, set fire to the premises one day at lunch before massacring seven people with an axe, and as far as anyone knows there was no known motive for the killings. Shortly after the murders Wright received a divorce from his first wife, Kitty Tobin, mother to six of his children (one of whom, as an adult, would invent Lincoln Logs), and married Miriam Noel, an artist and morphine addict, whom he divorced in less than a year to be with Olga Lazovich Hinzenberg, with whom he had one daughter, adopting another daughter from her previous marriage, Svetlana (whose widower, after she died many years later in a car accident, would coincidentally marry a second Svetlana, Joseph Stalin's daughter). It was a peculiar history, full of darkness and deceit, and one in which a cast of tragic female characters seems to serve as a titillating historical footnotes to an infamously wretched, incredibly talented male artist's enigmatic character. As we parked the car and walked through the main entrance of House on the Rock, O. and K. jointly explained a version of the building's origins: when Alex Jordan Jr. (an architect and the creator of the house) was young, they said, he drove drafts of a building he wished to construct to Taliesin in order to show them to Wright, his hero, from whom he desired approval. Instead Wright dismissed Jordan's designs outright saying he wasn't a capable architect and that Wright wouldn't have hired Jordan to "design a cheese crate or a chicken coop." As an act of revenge, O. and K. said, Jordan pointed to a spot along the horizon just above Wright's complex claiming he'd erect an even more elaborate, elegant home overlooking Taliesin and that he'd open it up to the public, charging admission. While in the midst of this story, a docent with long gray hair, emerald eye shadow, and a constellation of green sparkly buttons pinned to her sweater interrupted the guys to assert that *in fact* they were wrong. "I'm so sorry to interrupt," she said, before correcting them, but according to more recent research it seemed that Jordan would have been only nine years old during the time in which he supposedly met Wright and therefore could not have been personally rejected by the man, spoiling the rumor that the motivation for the house's construction was based in reaction, though I imagined it was still conceivable for Jordan to have felt he'd had something to prove to Wright, his idol—the most intimidating paternal figure in his field—as it is well known that one's most enduring relationships are not always authentic, and that we frequently fight our fiercest battles with the invented personalities that irrationally occupy our imaginations. In addition, the docent went on, during the years K. and O. had mentioned, Wright was not living in Spring Green, Wisconsin, but based in Japan where he was constructing the Imperial Hotel. This second version of the story was clearly correct, though I still preferred the first for, like many, I favor narratives that please me (in this case,

that the house was part of a long-term plot for artistic revenge)
more than those that depict reality; this preference is problem-
atic, and it is most likely our reckless capacity for ignoring evidence that will ultimately destroy the human species. O. and K.
thanked the woman and we moved on, circling the newly created lobby, which had been made into a miniature museum of
sorts with plaques and informative pamphlets announcing
quick details about the house: its public opening in 1959; the
fact that for decades a barely mentioned woman named Gladys
Welsh managed all of the business, correspondence, and ac-
counting in addition, so said the sign, to the emotional needs
of her "mercurial" boss; and further information about where
Alex Jordan Jr. went to grade school. After a few paragraphs I
turned away, preferring not to know too much before entering.
I would almost always rather experience something before being told about it, and despise the sense of déjà vu or echoing
affirmation prelude provides, I rarely consult reviews before
encountering a work and often refuse to read a book if the plot
has been detailed aggressively. I waited years, for example, to
pick up a novel by Roberto Bolaño because I had been the re-
cipient of so much commentary concerning his books (and
*how much I'd like them*) from enthusiastic male friends, and for
the same reason I have yet to watch *Making a Murderer*, a Net-
flix documentary about a wrongful conviction in Wisconsin (in
which the characters supposedly have a north country dialect
similar to branches of my family—"hey der" or "why'dja go do
dat den?"), and maybe I never will. As we exited the museum I
knew little besides what K. and O. had told me as well as the
basic fact, mentioned on a plaque, that the house rests on Deer
Shelter Rock, a jagged ridge above the Driftless hills,

information that could be discerned by its exterior appearance. I snapped a photo of a panel K. pointed to and we turned around, handing tickets to our docent friend and beginning the tour. The first section took us through the house; we ambled up narrow hallways with stone floors and stone walls, winding, as if hiking, up and around, disturbed only by episodic patches of carpet and interior decorating. In what was laid out as a living room there were replica Tiffany lamps, inky dragon paintings, damp slate slabs, and ornamental rugs. I immediately thought of Wright's Fallingwater in Pennsylvania—the influence was obvious—where I had attended a wedding months before and witnessed the tight corridors, corner cubbies, dark features, and East Asian influences that are associated with Wright's aesthetic. Jordan's house seemed at first overwhelmingly similar to what I had seen at Fallingwater but then, just as quickly, it was not; this house was coarser, gloomier, less careful, like encountering a creepy tree fort or beatnik's lair grafted onto a cave wall. We moved slowly. New to the experience, I pointed out each enchanting or mysterious detail not realizing there would be approximately three hours and several buildings' worth of ludicrous trinkets and insane bucolic panoramas. Like Alice's astonishment while falling down the rabbit hole, I failed to predict the awe I was to discover at the bottom. *Am I inside or outside?* I asked K.—an old joke that referenced my perpetual spatial confusion. The three of us sat awkwardly on a couch as a stranger took our picture. As we climbed higher and higher through winding passages and clammy quarters replete with stained glass displays and a player piano, brass ornaments and gaudy baubles, red reflections and shag textures, we eventually neared an entrance to something labeled the "Infinity Room," which turned out to be a 218-foot constricting hallway, a bridge to nowhere stretching out into the sky with thousands of windows but no underlying support beams, coming to a gradual point as if the room was a tapering gang plank. O., notoriously afraid of heights, refused to step out so K. and I tiptoed as far as we could bear, hovering floors above the peaceful Wisconsin woods where, if one crept toward the edge, they could make out the faint burble of creek water and staccato birdsong. The room, although vowing to be *infinite* was obviously not, for as we know everything in this universe halts—or at least turns—evolving toward some new, previously unpredictable future and making our human symbols of eternity vital, absurd, and soothing. I admired Jordan's optimism, his impulse to construct a room that demonstrated the romance of infinity by causing its viewers to float free, cloud-like above the ground, and it was the first of many times that day I understood the compound to be an expression of hope, proof that one could accumulate and revise for an entire lifetime however eccentric the practice might appear to outsiders. What happened for the next three hours is hard to describe: room after room of dubious junk, theater props, outrageous sculptures, and obsessive collections. In a section called "Streets of Yesterday"—which imitated an old-timey late-nineteenth-century village, as if one was stepping onto the set of *Our Town*—there were glass cabinets with multiple sizes of jeweled Fabergé eggs; an enclosed tableau of a Dalmatian, a wooden table, fireman's helmet, and the remains of a poker game; hand-painted signs for snake oils and nostrums ("Dr. Hammond's Nerve and Brain Pills," "Dr. Rose's Arsenic Complexion Wafers," "Dr. Kilmer's Female Remedy"); cabinets of blue and yellow blown-glass vases; silver tea kettles; ornate plates; robotic fortune tellers; fire trucks; electric weight belts; shelves of miniature porcelain faunae; a series of cartoonish piggy banks; and something called "The Gladiator," a life-sized marionette musical act backed by a "Colossal!, Gigantic!" calliope with wires tugging the arms of a wooden mannequin hitting a snare drum in perfect rhythm. There were weapons, dragons, and dolls, figurines and ancient mythological references. The place was like a maze with an extended center and even if one wished to flee they couldn't really, as there was only one very limited path forward and it was practical, even for the uncomfortable, to continue in the same direction they had started in, doomed to loop the labyrinth and experience every last charm or made-scene. Jordan's construction held his viewer's attention hostage causing one to *ooh* and *ahh* as if visiting a friend's new home or babysitting a child with favorite toys: *Well, look at that! Isn't it beautiful! Show me more!* It was obvious that the collector of these items was oppressed by a deep and troubling lack of control, a need to possess one of everything, a desire to be the cause of his and everyone else's *wonder*. Elements of the erratic and elegant design reminded me of other unusual Midwestern architectural compositions such as the Grotto of the Redemption, the largest grotto in the world, built steadily over the course of forty-two years by Father Paul Dobberstein in West Bend, Iowa, as an offering to the Virgin Mary for healing him of pneumonia in his youth; or perhaps the Dickeyville Grotto, not far away, in southwest Wisconsin, which brags shrines to Christopher Columbus, George Washington, and Abraham Lincoln; or even Indiana's Ultraviolet Apocalypse Grotto, host of a black-light archangel Gabriel. To me, no matter how dazzling, these garish spiritual structures appear aggressive (are there grottos made by women?) but I will confess that I have always adored Kurt Schwitters's *Merzbau*, a three dimensional multi-modal construction in which the ceilings and walls of Schwitters's Hannover, Germany home were deliberately transformed into a grotto-like space via the accumulation of collaged layers, nooks and caverns, stalactites and stalagmites, and plaster limbs protruding from dangerous angles resulting in an always-altering "living sculpture" that could only permanently exist in one's memory of a former state of its being. "I am a painter and I nail my pictures together," announced Schwitters in his 1918 Dadaist-debut interview. *Merzbau*, his life's work, was in constant flux, an autobiography that coiled in on and interrupted itself, constricting the physical flexibility of its domestic inhabitants (when looking at the few remaining photos I always wonder how his children felt about living in such a confining space) and ornamented with themed pockets—drawings, patchworks, effigies—that would be concealed or revealed by additional bulges, refrains, erasures, and paintings. The engine of the piece was *continuation*; concepts would disappear as they developed, buried below the surface, never to be seen again, or were alternately excavated as the sculpture shifted organically. In 1937, almost twenty years after its initial construction, *Merzbau* was destroyed in an Allied bombing raid shortly after Schwitters and his family fled to Norway; he created a second version there, which was abandoned during a Nazi raid and later burned down, and a third in England that was left incomplete upon his death in 1948 and is currently the only version to be restored by preservationists and accessible to the public. We turned a corner into the next section of the House on the Rock, a factory-sized warehouse called "The Heritage of the Sea," in the center of which rested the blimp-sized figure of a sea monster battling a giant squid adjacent to a yellow-jacketed man in an almost-capsized rowboat riding fake waves while a whale boat sat shipwrecked inside the mouth of the monster. "But... *Why*??..." I asked the guys, desperate, as they grinned at my bewilderment. It was a lot to process and, looking back, this might have been the instant I understood one should resist their first two urges upon entering this tourist trap: to bring children, or to take psychedelics. This room, although huge, had strictly controlled pathways with some sections hovering a hundred feet above the ground, supported with rickety walkways and feeble railings. The infrastructure was airy and weak with the atmosphere of an old roller coaster in which one is left to guess whether the ride's been recently fortified; it would have been simple for someone to topple over the side of a barrier to an untimely and idiotic death. In any case, after encountering the baffling blimp-sized seafaring squid and its exhaustive side-wonders (collections of toy tall ships; boats in bottles; walls of fisherman knots; whale vertebrae; yellowed tusks with etched tableau; oil orca paintings; ancient maps; horse thief posters; pocket telescopes; a series of multisized brass compasses, globes; ear bones; sponge skeletons; and a carved nude mermaid extending out of an oak barrel), we entered an equally enigmatic barn-sized chamber crowded with hot air balloons, crescent moons, and stars sinking from the ceiling; a gold and red horse-drawn carriage; crosses and animated string-puppets; Burma Shave signage ("he lit a match / to check gas tank / that's why / they call him / skinless Frank"); jeweled and feathered masquerade costumes; the "Throne of

Passion," a carnivalesque desire-tester (lighting up with fates of "sexy," "wild," "loveable," "out of control," or "brain-dead"); antique shotguns; stained glass montages; miniature toy vehicles (fire trucks, a Model T auto, delivery cars for Pork 'n' Beans, Budweiser, Mobile, and S&F Toys); a massive blinking fluorescent pizza man sign (the air suddenly thick with the scent of mozzarella and pepperoni!?!?), and a working Rube Goldberg machine with a panel reminding one that the contraption is a "contrivance that brings about by complicated means what apparently can be accomplished simply") before progressing into another veritable ocean of nostalgia featuring a series of striking vintage no-player instruments called the "Music of Yesterday: Presenting the Magnificent Machines of a Magnificent Era," requiring House on the Rock–branded coins to provoke their ghost songs. The melodies were brash and irritating, causing a racket similar to that which I'd once heard in a viral video called "Orchestra Fail," shown to me by my brother M., which portrayed a high school ensemble performing a painfully out-of-tune version of the theme from *2001: A Space Odyssey*, all awkward squeaks and amusingly unsynchronized cymbals. In this exhibit one could witness hundreds of self-playing organs, violins, accordions, flutes, harps, and horns, organized in such a way that they would execute their given measure of a well-known song or symphony. The rooms were dusty and dark with floral wallpaper, haphazard chandeliers, cartoon statues of grimacing villains, flashy furniture, gold trim, room-based color themes ("The Blue Room," "The Red Room," etc.), and even a wall-sized music box. Several hours into this journey, feeling irrevocably *committed*, I appreciated that what had begun in my case as a simple honeymoon tourist attraction was now the stifling nightmare of my waking life. Each grimy music machine's glory sounded less like a celebration and more like a funeral dirge. When we entered The Red Room I walked deliberately down the narrow aisle with K. by my side while O. waited near the front, plugging coins into the slots, and Tchaikovsky's "Dance of the Sugar Plum Fairy" began to intensify. Everything in the room sparkled, the music was bright, and we stared in delight as the instruments—arranged by some long-ago feat of algorithm and puppetry—plucked their own strings, making it easy to imagine that after the building closed each night these contraptions practiced at their own pace. Standing in that crimson chamber, regaled by machines, I felt the three of us were complicit in some ancient ritual. There was the timelessness of the music and a veil of dust blessing everything. There was the sense that we'd been here before and would return again. Perhaps it was this trance state that led me to recall one winter night when I was young—twenty or perhaps twenty-one—when, while sleeping in a small bed in a small apartment not far from here in Madison, I'd had a dream extraordinary enough that over a decade later I still knew the details. I dreamt that I was ill with a disease that caused deep coughs and a spiking fever, a tense chest and numb limbs, and that the diagnosis was fatal. My then-boyfriend, T.—who was sleeping beside me—performed an approximate version of himself in the narrative, offering to walk to the nearest pharmacy in the middle of a blizzard to procure the necessary medicine. Would T. find the cure in time? Would I die? And then something was waking me. T. muttered "What kind?" and I stared for a moment at his sleeping profile before nodding off again. The following morning T. explained that in *his* dream he was standing in an aisle at Walgreens asking me what brand of medicine to buy. This plot transference was baffling and in the years that have passed I have found the experience to belong to a small set of occurrences that are utterly incomprehensible and, in all of their magic, *unrepeatable*, although I recognize that when referring to a dream *nothing had happened*. We believe we understand the world more than we do, and in a quest for logic force discrete, unimportant images into what become our most noteworthy stories. There is perhaps no better example of this than the art of dream interpretation, which demonstrates how humans think they can predict the future or comprehend the past, confusing a meaningless series of images with insight. The trouble often occurs when one can't determine where the dream begins and their waking life ends. *Are we inside or outside? Are we small or far away?* As a child I had epic nightmares: wars and legends, the intricate politics of fabricated nations. Once when I was in high school I remember my father waking in the middle of the night to a noise that turned out to be my brother P., maybe fourteen, slowly filling every concave object in our kitchen with tap water. My father discovered all of the downstairs surfaces covered with pots and pans and bowls and buckets and P., standing at the faucet, both hard at work and sleeping. Supposedly Mary Shelley conceived of the characters in *Frankenstein* while dreaming; she wrote, "When I placed my head on my pillow, I did not sleep, nor could I be said to think. My imagination, unbidden, possessed and guided me, gifting the successive images that arose in my mind a vividness far beyond the usual bounds of reverie." When I thought of the overlapping dream with T., I wondered if I could ever be that close to someone again—if youthful intimacy is even what caused it. As we entered the most famous exhibit in the House on the Rock—the room with the indoor carousel—it was difficult to recall how I had arrived here, in this place, and why these two particular men were escorting me. We saw tigers and ostriches, giraffes, zebras, eagles, unicorns, elephants, elk, dragons, mountain lions, and mermaids—a menagerie in bright colors with shiny enamel skin, lit in such a way as to make them blaze as they spun through the dark room. A plaque reported that the carousel contained 269 animals, 182 chandeliers, over 20,000 lights, zero horses, and that the whole thing was worth several million dollars. One would guess that the noisy performance would be hell for the sole staff member assigned to stand guard at the side of the room, but he was friendly, pulling out his earplugs to compliment "Alex's" vision. We gaped in amazement, yelling to each other over the jaunty tune. Covering the ceiling were hundreds of barely clothed mannequin angels with enormous feathered wings sailing together—as if an army of synchronized swimmers—in one direction toward the only exit, which was shaped like the mouth of a fire-breathing demon. There had been so many coincidences. So many ways we had looped without realizing. At our wedding reception my mother had said that, unbeknownst to me, the Lake Geneva hotel we were headed to was the one she and my father had attempted to go to after their wedding. My parents' best friend, P., for whom my brother is named, showed up and spent the better part of a week with them. The place where O. and I were staying in Madison—built in 1948 on the Lake Mendota side of the isthmus—was, it turned out, where my maternal grandparents first met. I imagined that the carousel's giraffe, in its endless revolutions, saw thousands of tourists a day and then, every few years, encountered the same face as part of the rotation. Do we live more than once? If so, I'd return to Madison, to the Crystal Corner with friends, chatting with our favorite bartender. But we don't always get to choose what we return to. We finished the tour, stepping outside and into the sunlight like waking into another life. When O. and I returned to the hotel we watched out our window as a few college boys dashed over the cracked frozen web of Lake Mendota, sans fear, before we headed to the "relaxation pool," some combination of hot tub and bubble bath. Purple strobe lights bobbed along the wall like an aquarium disco. About an hour later—*was I inside or outside? was I warm or cool?*—we went to change out of our swimsuits and as I exited the women's locker room I found—in the place where O. should have been—another man leaning against the wall, watching chlorinated water effervesce through a small glass window. He asked me where I was from and about the view from my room. Had I eaten in the new restaurant? We spoke for a minute and then—while looking into my eyes in such a way that I could see he was deciding something—the man launched into a story: "You know," he said, tossing an embroidered hotel towel over his shoulder, "I'll tell you something. It was the strangest set of circumstances that brought me here. . . ."

# Acknowledgments

Thank you to the following editors for publishing versions of these essays: Sven Birkerts at *AGNI*; Liz Johnston at *Brick: A Literary Journal*; Janice Lee at *Entropy*; Andy Fitch at Essay Press; Andrew Malan Milward at *Mississippi Review*; Gabriel Blackwell at *The Rupture* (formerly *The Collagist*); and Rachel Abramowitz at *Wave Composition*.

Thank you to those who appear as characters in these essays and to those who shared their stories, sometimes more than once, as well as the friends and family who supported the writing of this book via their conversation, wit, and wisdom: Margaret Pagel, Paul Pagel, Liz Pagel, Mike Pagel, Lauren Keith, Elle Pagel, Ivy Pagel, Les Pagel, Abby Pagel, Emily Pettit, Amber Dermont, Lauren Haldeman, Zach Savich, Jane Lewty, Dora Malech, Danny Khalastchi, Vinnie Wilhelm, Stephen Lovely, Amy Margolis, Kiki Petrosino, Mary Hickman,

Josh Fomon, Catina Bacote, Michelle Taransky, Dan Beachy-Quick, Sevy Perez, Zach Isom, Sarah Minor, Krysia Orlowski, Leora Fridman, Mike Geither, Imad Rahman, the bar night crew, and the #lakelife crowd.

Thank you to my colleagues and students at Cleveland State University, the NEOMFA, the Cleveland State University Poetry Center, and Rescue Press. Thank you to the Cleveland State University Faculty Scholarship Initiative Award and the Ohio Arts Council for support during the writing of this book.

Thank you to Joanna Ruocco, Dan Waterman, Johnathan Berry, and everyone at FC2 and The University of Alabama Press for your work and enthusiasm. Thank you to Hanif Abdurraqib, Barbara Browning, and Sabrina Orah Mark for your generosity.

Thank you to the people and places who lent me space to write in: Emily Pettit, Rick Kenney and Carol Light, Marvin and Dorothy Bell, Shoals Marine Labs, the Headlands Center for the Arts, and the Hermitage Artist Retreat.

Thank you to Ossian, Winter, and Satchel.

Thank you most of all to Madeline McDonnell, Kevin González, Lauren Shapiro, James Shea, and Alyssa Perry for reading drafts of this manuscript and chatting through them. Thank you to Hilary Plum for your friendship, your writing, and for making everything more interesting.

# Notes

The quotes which appear in "Driving at Night: A Chorus" are from the following texts:

WebMD's 2009 article "Eye Health Center: LASIK Eye Surgery;" the Oxford English Dictionary; Deborah Blum's *Ghost Hunters*; C.D. Broad's *Lectures on Psychical Research*; Emily Dickinson's *Selected Letters*; Hilda Doolittle's "Tribute to the Angels;" Ralph Waldo Emerson's "Circles" and "Experience;" William Fish's *Perception, Hallucination, and Illusion*; Alan Gauld's *The Founders of Psychical Research*; Edmund Gurney, Frederic W. H. Myers, and Frank Podmore's *Phantasms of the Living*; Renee Haynes's *The Society for Psychical Research, 1882–1982*; William James's "What Psychical Research Has Accomplished (1892);" Henry Wadsworth Longfellow's "My Lost Youth;" Claudius Ptolemy's *Optics*, as referenced in Nicholas J.

Wade's *A Natural History of Vision*; and Edith Wharton's "The Eyes."

# Image Credits

**Lost in Thought**

Von Humboldt, Alexander. *Dragon Tree of Orotava*. Engraving. 1810. Public domain.

Callahan, Harry. *Untitled (#1)*. 1950. Silver gelatin print. © The Estate of Harry Callahan, courtesy Pace/MacGill Gallery, New York.

Callahan, Harry. *Untitled (#8)*. 1950. Silver gelatin print. © The Estate of Harry Callahan, courtesy Pace/MacGill Gallery, New York.

Pagel, Caryl. *Milwaukee Avenue (Chicago)*. Photograph. 2012.

*Eusapia Palladino performs a séance, 1890s*. Photograph. Public Domain.

Rudd, Scott. *Marina Abramović performing* The Artist Is Present *at the Museum of Modern Art, New York*. Photograph. 2010. Courtesy of Scott Rudd Photography.

## A Pickle for the Knowing Ones

Pagel, Caryl. *Libertyville Football Practice #1*. Photograph. 2013.

Pagel, Caryl. *Libertyville Football Practice #2*. Photograph. 2013.

Dexter, Lord Timothy. *A Pickle for the Knowing Ones, or Plain Truth In a Homespun Dress*. 1802. Public domain.

*CEN-DeadProposal-03, Alexey Bykov with fiancé*. Central European News. 2012.

Matta-Clark, Gordan. *Splitting*. Photograph. 1974. © 2019 Estate of Gordon Matta-Clark / Artists Rights Society (ARS), New York.

Pagel, Caryl. *Libertyville High School Sign*. Photograph. 2013.

## Alphabet

LJNova Scotia. *Uterus*. Pixabay. Public Domain.

Rohm, Robert. *Rope Piece*. 1969. With permission from Candy Adriance and Chuck Mayer.

Pagel, Caryl. *Utah Fence*. Photograph. 2014

Pagel, Caryl. *Satchel and O*. Photograph. 2014.

Pagel, Caryl. *Spiral Jetty*. Photograph. 2014.

## What Remains To Be Seen

Truesdell, Nathan. *Balloonfest*. Film. 2017. Still shots of balloons in net.

Truesdell, Nathan. *Balloonfest*. Film. 2017. Still shots of Terminal Tower and balloon release.